psalms 365

DEVELOP A LIFE OF WORSHIP AND PRAYER

VOLUME I

ENDORSEMENTS

The main body parts for reading the Bible aren't the eyes and brain; it's the hands and feet. This theme is woven throughout *Psalms 365*. As it should be! The focus on living the Word, or as James puts it, "doing it" (James 1:25) is what makes this study in the Psalms top-notch.
—Dr. Lawson Murray, President, Scripture Union Canada

Over the years the psalms have become a great source of hope. David Kitz's devotions are a great accompaniment to them. I find his writing both insightful and uplifting.
—Alan Kearns, Glenrothes, Scotland

This is a delightful daily devotional for those of us who want to enhance our reading of the Psalms. David Kitz does an excellent job of relating our realities to the Psalmist's engagement with God through the ups and downs of life. His keen insights undergird the guided responses to living fully in the light of the God we love.
—Steve Falkiner, President, Canadian Foursquare Gospel Church

In his devotional reflections, David Kitz plumbs the depths of the rich treasure of the Psalms in ways that are not only insightful, but very relevant and applicable, addressing the blessings and challenges of walking in the Lord's ways. A very helpful resource for anyone's personal devotional use.
—Rev. Daryl Solie, Lutheran Pastor

I have been an online follower of David Kitz for several years now. His interpretation, his historical knowledge, and his ability to give every day practical experience through the Psalms has been inspiring and extremely useful for me personally. David takes the words from Scripture and gives them new insight for today's world. His book, *Psalms 365* is a strong devotional handbook for living a Christian life.

—**Kathy Boecher**, Christian blogger, playwright, poet, and humorist

David Kitz and his wide-ranging talent as an author are both unique. His devotional posts on the Psalms arrive daily for his subscribers. It is a delight to know they will now be available in book format. In these pages, readers can find much inspiration and insight.

—**Hon. David Kilgour**, D. Div (hon), Minister of State (Canada)

What a great tonic for my day-to-day walk with God! Like a daily regimen of vitamins and minerals, *Psalms 365* by my friend David Kitz has invigorated my start to each day. I believe it is also fortifying my mind and spirit for all the challenges my life will bring in the years to come. Creatively written, biblically insightful, and immensely practical, this must-have compendium to Psalms is timely and life-giving.

—**Lyle Johnson**, Founder and President, Nextlevel Ministries

David Kitz writes with a heart that wants to worship God, and he invites us all to join in through his writings. His daily reflections on the Psalms are practical and make you want to love our God and Savior more.

—**Jimmy Li**, pastor & blogger for Veritas Domain

For more than twenty years, David Kitz has been my friend, colleague, and fellow member in a weekly men's fellowship group. He has always demonstrated his passion to know and make manifest God's Word in his life, to draw close to the heart of his Father. In other words, he is a man after God's own heart, which is so clearly evident in this new daily devotion book. I have had the distinct privilege of reading these devotions through David's blog in preparation for this new publication. Each devotion will inspire and provide the reader with biblical insights and life applications, through a daily call to prayer, worship, obedience, thanksgiving, and meditation on God's Word. May this book help to strengthen, heal, and encourage all who read it!

—Don MacGregor, leader, Next Level Ministries

Psalms 365

DEVELOP A LIFE OF WORSHIP AND PRAYER

VOLUME I

DAVID KITZ

PUBLISHING THE POSITIVE
Plymouth, Massachusetts

Cover and Interior Design: Derinda Babcock

Editor(s): Sue Fairchild, Susan K. Stewart, Deb Haggerty

Author Represented By: Credo Communications, LLC

PUBLISHED BY: Elk Lake Publishing, Inc., 35 Dogwood Drive, Plymouth, MA 02360, 2020

Library Cataloging Data

Names: Kitz, David (David Kitz)

Psalms 365: Develop a Life of Biblical Worship and Prayer—Volume 1 / David Kitz

262 p. 23cm × 15cm (9in × 6 in.)

Identifiers: ISBN-13: 978-1-64949-108-4 (paperback) | 978-1-64949-109-1 (trade paperback)

| 978-1-64949110-7- (e-book)

Key Words: inspirational, devotional, prayer, praise, worship, Christian living, relationship with God

LCCN: 2020950700 Nonfiction

DEDICATION

This book is dedicated to my sisters Georgina, Edith, Edna, and Donna, and my brother Dale.

TABLE OF CONTENTS VOLUME 1

FOREWORD

Come and see what the LORD has done! (Psalm
46:8)

There is a year's worth of discipleship training between the
covers of this three-volume set. Perhaps I should say a lifetime's
worth. Not the kind we usually think of, with instructions to
"Do this" and "You need to do that." This is a book that greets
you where you are and offers you a hand as you cross rivers,
climb mountains, and travel through dark valleys in your walk
with God.

David Kitz is not afraid to speak openly of his own mountains
and valleys. He speaks in the same way the first David—and
other psalm-writers—speak. You will read words from his
personal experience, from the heart, and out of a profound daily
journey with his Lord. He often expands what the psalmist says
to include what we know now that Jesus has come, things of
which the psalmists caught glimpses, things "into which angels
long to look." He takes us there.

Kitz writes with insight and with imagination. This isn't
a book of "comforting thoughts" with which to begin your
day. It will inspire you, yes, but it will also challenge you and
encourage you to take an honest look at yourself, always in the
light of Jesus, who loves you.

When the first disciples met Jesus for the first time, they
asked him where he was staying. His answer: "Come and see"
(John 1:37-38).

Yes, come and see. Come and see Jesus within the Psalms
and within these pages.

—**Annabel Robinson**, Publications Manager, Scripture
Union Canada

AN INTRODUCTION TO THE PSALMS

For nearly three thousand years, people have been getting in touch with God through the sacred literature of the book of Psalms. Generation after generation has drawn strength, comfort, and inspiration from the words of the psalmist.

There are one hundred fifty psalms in the book of Psalms, and one of the most remarkable things about them is their emotional span. They range from giddy heights of joy and praise to great depths of depression and sorrow. The full array of human emotion and experience is on display. Whatever state you find yourself in, there's a psalm for that—a psalm for every situation and human need. If you are in desperate straits, there's a psalm for that. If you are soaring in the presence of God, there's a psalm for that too. The Psalms reflect our need for God and our desire to connect with him in all of life's experiences.

There's something innately powerful about good literature. The characters and events we read about become very real to us. We come to know the people introduced on the page. Their experiences become our own. This is true of the Psalms as well. The Psalms have passed the test of time. They represent the best in sacred literature.

In times of calamity, the Psalms bring peace. When storms rage within, a psalm can provide a haven of rest. When anger erupts, a psalm can act as a release valve. When God seems distant, the Psalms bring us near.

Psalms 365 is a devotional study that guides the reader through the entire book of Psalms during a full year. My goal is to help the reader interact with each psalm and connect with God in a fresh and living way.

There is something surprisingly practical about the Psalms. They are meant to be lived. The Bible is, in fact, a living document that must be applied to life to be effective. This should not surprise us since, "The word of God is living and active" (Hebrews 4:12a). During this study, we will draw from a range of biblical sources and real-life experiences to help the Psalms come alive.

There is power in the unchanging Word of God. My prayer is that you will experience that power for yourself. May you discover Jesus, the Good Shepherd, walking off the pages of the Psalms and into your life.

As never before, let the Psalms come alive for you.

DAY 1: THE TREE OF LIFE

TODAY'S READING: PSALM 1

KEY VERSE: PSALM 1:3

That person is like a tree planted by streams of water, which yields its fruit in season and whose leaf does not wither—whatever they do prospers.

REFLECTION

Have you ever noticed the prominent role trees play in the Bible? The creation account in Genesis begins with God planting two very special trees in the Garden of Eden: The Tree of Life and the Tree of the Knowledge of Good and Evil. After our first parents' disobedience, we were banned from access to the Tree of Life. But the amazing, good news of the Bible arrives at the end of the book. In the last chapter of the book of Revelation, God restores our access to the Tree of Life (Revelations 22:1–5).

In a very real sense, the Bible is a story about trees.

In the very first psalm, the life of the righteous is compared to a fruit-bearing tree, flourishing by streams of water. The psalmist presents a picture of tranquil beauty. Does that peaceful picture describe our lives? Sometimes, I feel more like windblown chaff—rather worthless and lacking a sense of direction.

But that's where the other tree at the heart of the Bible comes into play. This tree stands on a hill called Calvary. There our Savior bled and died. There he showed us our true worth. There our sins were washed away, never to be remembered again. Calvary is where we became righteous, not by works we've done, but solely by the grace and forgiveness of Christ.

What a beautiful tree! The tree on Mount Calvary isn't beautiful because of its leaves. This tree is beautiful because of its fruit—the fruit of redemption purchased by the blood of Jesus. Our righteousness is solely due to him.

RESPONSE:

Dear Lord Jesus, thank you for your sacrifice. Help me to always remember you are the true source of my righteousness. At your prompting, help me to rid myself of the worthless chaff in my life. Wind of God, blow on me. Water of life, refresh my soul. May I be fruitful, Lord, for you. Amen.

YOUR TURN:

Have you knelt before the tree on Mount Calvary? Today, how can you show your appreciation for the tree God planted there?

DAY 2: KISS THE SON

TODAY'S READING: PSALM 2

KEY VERSE: PSALM 2:12

Kiss his son, or he will be angry and your way will lead to your destruction, for his wrath can flare up in a moment. Blessed are all who take refuge in him.

REFLECTION

Kisses are close-up and personal, so intimate. I don't know about you, but I don't kiss everyone I meet. Kisses are reserved for those special people in my life—people I know and trust. People I love.

Here in Psalm 2, kings and rulers are commanded to kiss the Son of God. What an odd command. What is the significance of this? The kiss in this case signals full submission to the supreme potentate. Kings and rulers are to submit to the overarching rule of Christ over themselves, their affairs, and their entire domain.

Psalm 2 is the first of several messianic psalms scattered throughout the book of Psalms. There is nothing subtle about the messianic message found here. The Lord has installed his anointed as king in Zion and, furthermore, this anointed one is identified as the Son of God. The term the Lord's "anointed" is frequently translated as Messiah or Christ.

In the book of Acts, we see the apostles viewed this psalm as the prophetic fulfillment of Christ's mission during his last days in Jerusalem. The anointed Son of God was rejected by Herod and Pilate, the rulers of that time. They refused to kiss the Son (see Acts 4:23–31).

But what about me? Have I kissed the Son? Have I submitted to his will for my life? In my own small way, I am also a monarch, a ruler of my own domain. Today, will I allow him to rule over me, my conduct, my activities, and my financial affairs?

RESPONSE

Dear Lord Jesus, thank you for your unconditional love. You want only the best for me. I yield to you. Help me to embrace your will and purpose for my life. I trust in you. I love you, Lord. With my lips I kiss the Son. Amen.

YOUR TURN

Have you kissed the Son? How can you show your love and loyalty to Jesus today?

DAY 3: CONFIDENCE DURING ADVERSITY

TODAY'S READING: PSALM 3

KEY VERSE: PSALM 3:3

But you, LORD, are a shield around me, my glory,
the One who lifts my head high.

REFLECTION

When do you most need God?

The answer to that question is easy—when I'm in deep trouble. It's natural to call out to God when I'm in some great or urgent need. An anonymous returning veteran from the First World War said it best, "There are no atheists in the trenches. When the artillery shells start exploding to the right and left, even atheists discover how to pray."

The context of Psalm 3 is of great significance. David finds himself in the midst of a life-threatening tragedy. He is fleeing from his palace in the nation's capital because his son is conspiring to murder him and seize the kingdom from his hands. Here is the great delta—the extreme low point in David's life.

How does David respond? With utter confidence in God! Yes, he calls out to the Lord for deliverance, but he does so with complete assurance God will answer. There isn't the slightest hint of doubtful desperation in his voice. Having prayed to the Lord, he boasts in his ability to sleep, because he knows God will answer.

How could David be so confident—so self-assured? Actually, David's assurance rested entirely on the Lord, not on himself. David had a wealth of experience with God. In his mind, the Lord was tried, tested, and true through the ups and downs of life.

He knew something we need to know. God will come through. He will bring salvation and deliverance!

RESPONSE

Lord God, save me from all my troubles. I put my confidence in you. You reach down to me at the low points in my life. You have never abandoned me. Amen.

YOUR TURN

Take a moment to reflect on the goodness of the Lord. Has he saved you from deep trouble in the past?

DAY 4: THE SHINING FACE

Today's Reading: Psalm 4

Key Verse: Psalm 4:6

Many, LORD, are asking, "Who will bring us prosperity?" Let the light of your face shine on us.

REFLECTION

Where are you looking?

Think about this statement for a moment: Where you look is where you go. If you are walking, presumably you are looking where you are going. If you are driving, you are looking where you are going. If your eyes are distracted in either of these situations, your journey will certainly come to an abrupt end. As you move through your day—as you move through life—where you look is where you go.

If you look to the internet for porn, you are sure to find and be trapped by it. If you look to television for entertainment, you are sure to find it. If you don't take care, that entertainment, in more subtle ways, can ensnare and deaden your spirit. If you look to others, they will often disappoint you. As David points out in this psalm, all too often we "love delusions and seek false gods" (Psalm 4:2b). We are looking in the wrong places and consequently, we steer our life into the ditch.

In Psalm 4, David's approach is totally different. He is looking to the Lord, calling out to God. He fears the Lord (trembles and does not sin). In silence, he searches his heart and encourages us to do the same. Have you offered a sacrifice of righteousness recently? Right living has a cost. But it also pays enormous dividends.

As we trust in the Lord and look to him, as our loving Father, he turns his face to us. He fixes his gaze on us. The light of his face shines on us. Wow! That thought fills my heart with joy.

RESPONSE

Heavenly Father, today let the light of your face shine on me. Guide me in the way of truth. Light my path. I look to you, my Savior and my God. Amen.

YOUR TURN

Has the light of God's face shone on you recently? What was that like?

DAY 5: DOES GOD HEAR YOUR VOICE?

TODAY'S READING: PSALM 5:1–7

KEY VERSE: PSALM 5:3

In the morning, LORD, you hear my voice; in the morning I lay my requests before you and wait expectantly.

REFLECTION

Are you a morning person? Are you most productive in the morning hours, or do you revive after the sun sets? Our bodies move according to their own internal rhythm. Some people love to rise with the chirp of the first songbird, while others are true night owls. Often my wife catches her second wind in the evening as I'm fading into sweet oblivion.

David seems to be a morning person. Here in Psalm 5, we read these words from David: "In the morning, LORD, you hear my voice; in the morning I lay my requests before you and wait expectantly."

David was one of those early birds who began calling out to God at the break of day. He knew God listened. He made sure the Lord heard his voice.

Is the Lord hearing your voice in the morning? Are you calling out to him? Of course, your heavenly Father is pleased to hear your voice at any time, day or night. Is he familiar with your voice?

But there's more to this than just calling out to God and laying out your requests. David waits *expectantly*. He expects God to respond. He is listening, watching, and waiting for the Lord's reply. Have you built some wait time into your prayer time?

All too often our conversations with God are one-sided. We often simply blurt out our requests and rush off into our day. We don't wait expectantly for the Lord's reply as David did. We don't allow him time to respond.

RESPONSE

Heavenly Father, I call out to you. I lay out my requests. Teach me to wait expectantly for you. Open my ears to hear your voice. Amen.

YOUR TURN

Have you set aside a regular prayer time? What time works best for you?

DAY 6: LEAD ME, LORD

TODAY'S READING: PSALM 5:8–12

KEY VERSE: PSALM 5:8

Lead me, LORD, in your righteousness because of my enemies—make your way straight before me.

REFLECTION

How good is your eyesight? Is it 20/20? Tomorrow, I am going for an eye exam so that question has some personal relevance. I recently had elective lens replacement surgery. I simply got tired of wearing glasses. They were the bane of my childhood. In those early years, I was an active lad. I can't begin to count the number of times I broke or damaged the frames.

Going without glasses then was not an option. I was practically blind without my specs—everything was a blur.

Today's reading from Psalm 5 begins with David making this request: "Lead me, LORD, in your righteousness because of my enemies—make your way straight before me."

Trust me on this point. If you can't see clearly, you may need someone to lead you. David recognized his need. Because of his enemies, he needed the Lord to lead him. He knew his enemies were waiting to ambush him at any moment. But where were they? Enemies in hiding are not easily spotted. That's why, like David, we need the Lord. He sees everything.

My greatest enemies are not parading around out in the

open. They are lurking within. Pride and selfish ambition come dressed up in various disguises. As a man, it's easy to justify that lingering eye or that wayward glance. Somehow, we have 20/20 vision for that sort of thing. The truth is I need the Lord to lead me because of the enemies of my soul. How about you?

Now here is the outcome we want: "But let all who take refuge in you be glad; let them ever sing for joy. Spread your protection over them, that those who love your name may rejoice in you" (Psalm 5:11).

RESPONSE

Lord God, lead me. I can't see the dangers ahead. I am often unaware of the enemies trying to undermine my life and my love for you. Go before me. Show me the way, Lord Jesus, because you are the way. Amen.

YOUR TURN

How is your spiritual vision? Can you see the enemies that derail your progress?

DAY 7: A SOLUTION FOR SPIRITUAL CONSTIPATION

TODAY'S READING: PSALM 6

KEY VERSE: PSALM 6:6

I am worn out from my groaning. All night long I flood my bed with weeping and drench my couch with tears.

REFLECTION

The life of a God-follower isn't all happy days and sunny skies, as some preachers might have you believe. On the contrary, hard times and grief may frequent our way. Does that mean we are out of the will of God? Has God abandoned us during these times of inner turmoil, struggle, and hardship?

Judging by the life and experience of David as expressed through the Psalms, the answer is a resounding, "No." God has not abandoned you.

David met with God during his times of difficulty. He poured out his complaints before the Lord. He pleaded with God and held nothing back. Look at some of the keywords in this psalm: *agony, anguish, groaning, weeping, tears, and sorrow.* David experienced all these emotions. He didn't bottle them up. He poured them out before the Lord in prayer.

Many believers suffer from a form of spiritual constipation. They are filled with anger, hurt, and bitter disappointment. Life has been hard, but they are afraid to take their anguish before God. They put on a brave face for the world and the church, but inwardly they are dying. They need a massive dose of the Psalms of David—psalms of pouring out the heart. Fear not. God can handle your anguish and anger. He won't smite you dead for being honest about your feelings.

Are you hurt or feeling broken? Here is some sound advice. Take it to the Lord in prayer. Then take heart from what David says in the conclusion to this psalm, "The LORD has heard my cry for mercy; the LORD accepts my prayer" (Psalm 6:9).

RESPONSE

Dear God, I pour out my problems, hurts, and struggles before you. Hear my prayer. I know you are a God of mercy. I open myself to you. Amen.

YOUR TURN

Are you bottling up things that should be released to the Lord? Does heartfelt prayer bring relief?

DAY 8: TRANSPARENCY BEFORE GOD

TODAY'S READING: PSALM 7:1–9

KEY VERSE: PSALM 7:9

Bring to an end the violence of the wicked and make the righteous secure—you, the righteous God who probes minds and hearts.

REFLECTION

Have you ever been falsely accused? Have you been accused of wrongdoing by someone you consider a friend? That can be a deeply hurtful experience. In the context of this psalm, that's the situation David found himself in. He stands accused of repaying his ally with evil.

How did David respond? Did he strike down his accuser? Remember David is the king. He has the power to act—to unleash his vengeance. Would doing so be his just and righteous response? No, he takes his case before the Lord. In prayer, he declares, "Let the LORD judge the peoples" (Psalm 7:8). He invites God to judge him. He presents his case before "the righteous God who probes minds and hearts" (v. 9).

David was a man of God. He submitted his heart and mind to the all-seeing eye of God. He wanted the sin source cut off within him. Right thinking and righteous judgment begin when God and his Word gain entry to your heart.

Letting God handle our battles takes courage and integrity. What David did also took faith and transparency that men of position and power often lack today. Are you willing to let God probe your heart and your mind to find the guilty party? What might he find hidden away in the recesses of your mind and heart?

The writer of the book of Hebrews reminds us about the power of God's Word, "For the word of God is alive and active. Sharper than any double-edged sword, it penetrates even to dividing soul and spirit, joints and marrow; it judges the thoughts and attitudes of the heart" (Hebrews 4:12).

Let's willingly submit our hearts and minds to the all-seeing eye of God.

RESPONSE

Lord, I open my heart and my mind to your probing. I have nothing to hide, since you see all and know all, even the hidden things of the heart. Help me repent where needed. Amen.

YOUR TURN

Are you transparent before God? Why do we think we can hide something from God?

DAY 9: WILE E. COYOTE AND THE SCALES OF JUSTICE

TODAY'S READING: PSALM 7:10–17

KEY VERSE: PSALM 7:15–16

Whoever digs a hole and scoops it out falls into the pit they have made. The trouble they cause recoils on them; their violence comes down on their own heads.

REFLECTION

Ah justice, sweet justice. When we take justice into our own hands, it often has a boomerang effect. I am reminded of Wile E. Coyote and the roadrunner when I read these words from Psalm 7: "Whoever digs a hole and scoops it out falls into the pit they have made."

In those Saturday cartoons of my youth, poor Wile E. must have dug a hundred pits and fallen into them every time. Every clever scheme backfired catastrophically, and the roadrunner always escaped. To paraphrase the words of this psalm, *the trouble Wile E. caused recoiled on him; his violence came down on his own head.* Even now, can you picture the anvil falling on the hapless coyote as he lies in a crumpled heap at the bottom of the canyon? The cartoonist and the psalmist must have been reading from the same script!

Somehow, we often have the mistaken impression that getting even works—that scoring points at the expense of our neighbor elevates us. If snide sarcasm and putdowns elevate us, it's only the kind of elevation we often see in cartoons. Our clever remarks run us off the edge of a cliff, and like the cartoons, there we stand in the middle of thin air—the last one to realize we are heading down fast. That's justice, sweet justice, Psalm 7 style.

If as this psalm states, God "displays his wrath every day," it's only because we reap the reward of our sinful actions. In our selfishness, we harm instead of building up those around us. We try to pull ahead by pulling others down. This type of strategy is doomed to failure and always backfires. God and the roadrunner will see to that.

RESPONSE

Heavenly Father, today show me how I can build others up instead of tearing them down. I want to be more like you, Lord Jesus. You came to lift others up. In my interactions today, help me do the same. Amen.

YOUR TURN

Have you encouraged someone lately with a positive word? Did that bring a reward?

DAY 10: BIG GOD LITTLE ME

TODAY'S READING: PSALM 8

KEY VERSE: PSALM 8:1

LORD, our Lord, how majestic is your name in all the earth! You have set your glory in the heavens.

REFLECTION

There's something exquisitely beautiful about this psalm. We see the glory of the heavens, the sun, moon, and stars—the vast array of heavenly bodies. But there's more to this psalm than a pretty poetic picture of the heavens.

This psalm is about perspective. In the grand scheme of things, David grasps his true size—his insignificance. Beneath a canopy of stars, he has a transcendent moment—a God moment. He realizes the immensity of God. In the material realm, you and I are just a transitory flicker across the face of time. That's why David asks, "When I consider your heavens, the work of your fingers, the moon and the stars, which you have set in place, what is mankind that you are mindful of them, human beings that you care for them?" (Psalm 8:3–4). In the vastness of the universe, I am but a speck. Why would God even consider me?

But he does! That's the wonder of this psalm, and the wonder of our God. He is mindful of you and your concerns. God has crowned human beings—you and I—with glory and honor. When did that happen, you might ask?

Well, it happened at creation. God placed humankind

as the rulers of all creation. That's a huge responsibility—a responsibility we have often failed to fulfill. But God reaffirmed his love and commitment to us at the cross. Jesus considered you so significant that he bled and died for you. Now that's significance—eternal significance—in the face of God's own Son.

RESPONSE

Heavenly Father, creator of the universe, thank you for considering me. Thank you for being mindful of my daily concerns. I bring them to you, my majestic Lord. Amen.

YOUR TURN

Have you had a transcendent moment—a God moment? Write down how it happened and your thoughts about that moment.

DAY 11: THE WARRIOR KING

TODAY'S READING: PSALM 9

KEY VERSE: PSALM 9:10

Those who know your name trust in you, for you,
LORD, have never forsaken those who seek you.

REFLECTION

Without question, David was a man of war. After all,
this was the man who, as a strapping young teenager, slew
Goliath, the gigantic champion of the Philistines. Later,
David led King Saul's army as they charged into battle
with the enemies of Israel. Eventually, when David became
king, he secured Israel's borders and greatly expanded its
territory through conquest. David knew a few things about
bloodshed and war, and he had more than a few enemies.

Therefore, we should not be surprised that the language
of warfare and talk of enemies and destruction should appear
in the psalms that David wrote. He wrote, sang, and spoke
of the things he knew and experienced. He was personally
involved in life and death struggles. Consequently, he was
a man of violence, who lived and survived through violent
times.

But he loved God. Sometimes reconciling the slay-
my-enemies David with the Lord-is-my-shepherd David is
difficult. It's as though two contradictory Davids live in
one body. But then I look at myself—deep within myself.
Am I any different? There are more than a few contradictory
elements at work within me. The real warfare is within the

human spirit. Will I yield to the Spirit of God, or to the foul spirit of this world, and my own selfish pride?

Like David, I simply need God. I need to praise and exalt him over all else. When I do that, I gain perspective—the right perspective. With David I can say, "Those who know your name trust in you, for you, LORD, have never forsaken those who seek you."

RESPONSE

I praise you, Lord, and I seek you. Along with David, I can say you have upheld me in difficult times. Be the master within me. "I will be glad and rejoice in you; I will sing the praises of your name, O Most High" (Psalm 9:2). Amen.

YOUR TURN

Have you yielded to the Lord? Is he winning the warfare within you?

DAY 12: ASSIGNING BLAME OR ASSIGNING PRAISE

TODAY'S READING: PSALM 9:11–20

KEY VERSE: PSALM 9:16

The LORD is known by his acts of justice; the wicked are ensnared by the work of their hands.

REFLECTION

If only life were easy. If only life was just and fair! But it isn't. Life is filled with struggles and difficulties. I'm not always treated fairly, nor are you. Here in verse thirteen of this Psalm, David cries out, "LORD, see how my enemies persecute me!" You can sense the frustration in his voice. Though additional words were not recorded, David might have added, "This isn't fair, LORD. You aren't being fair!"

Instead, David assigns blame where blame is due. He blames his troubles on his enemies—his human oppressors—not on the Lord. By way of contrast, David has nothing but praise for the Lord. In verse eleven, he declares, "Sing the praises of the LORD, enthroned in Zion; proclaim among the nations what he has done."

If the source of your affliction is human, why do you blame God? We need to always keep verse sixteen of this psalm in mind: "The LORD is known by his acts of justice." In this life, we may not always see God's justice prevail, but rest assured on that great final day, he will prevail. Ultimately, his justice will be seen and known by all.

In times of trouble, God is our source of help and strength. Human help may fail us. Friends may let us down. We can wrongly blame the Lord for our troubles, or we can run to him for help. In all our troubles, we must keep this promise in mind: "But God will never forget the needy; the hope of the afflicted will never perish" (Psalm 9:18).

RESPONSE

Lord, in times of trouble, you are my help. I lay my troubles and my requests before you. I wait expectantly for you. I praise you for your goodness to me even in difficult times. Amen.

YOUR TURN

Have you been blaming God rather than thanking him? Take some time to praise him today.

DAY 13: NO ROOM FOR GOD?

TODAY'S READING: PSALM 10:1–4

KEY VERSE: PSALM 10:4

In his pride the wicked man does not seek him;
in all his thoughts there is no room for God.

REFLECTION

As I write my thoughts on Psalm 10, snow is drifting down outside my window, and my mind returns to our recent rendezvous with Christmas. Ah, Christmas! I love the significance of the season—time spent with family and thoughts of a babe in a manger. But for many, the celebration of Christ's birth has become a mangled wreck—a gross distortion. For millions of people, this commercial bonanza is completely devoid of any spiritual meaning. The holiday has become nothing more than a buying and selling frenzy—a pursuit of trinkets signifying nothing of eternal value.

In Psalm 10, we see the deceptive signs—the misdirected signs of the Christmas season. We are hunted down by the top-level merchandisers of this world through clever marketing schemes. Perhaps you were caught in the schemes they devised this past year. Rather than being a season where we seek the Lord, we can fall into their traps. We can find ourselves boasting about the cravings of our heart instead of the Creator of our heart. As the psalmist says, we bless the greedy and in so doing, we revile the Lord.

The words of the psalmist ring true, "In his pride the wicked man does not seek him; in all his thoughts there is no room for God" (v. 4).

No room for God … in today's world? In a perverse way, this absence of God seems rather appropriate. There was no room for God in Bethlehem on the night Jesus was born. No room for God … no room for the Creator and Savior of the universe! That sounds insane, but we seem to live in a world gone mad.

For you and me, our holiday doesn't have to be that way. While there was no room for God incarnate in Bethlehem, the magi sought him. They were hungry to know more about this Redeemer of Israel, and they crossed deserts to reach him. They came to kneel and worship a baby in a manger. Regardless of the season, or the season of our lives, you and I can set our hearts to be God seekers. In this new year, let's set our hearts to seek after the Lord.

RESPONSE

Jesus, I seek after you. Open my eyes to see you at work. You are not distant from me in time or space. Show up in my world today. I wait expectantly for you. Amen.

YOUR TURN

Have you seen Jesus in others? How can you seek God throughout the week?

DAY 14: WHEN THERE IS NO ROOM FOR GOD

TODAY'S READING: PSALM 10:5–11

KEY VERSE: PSALM 10:11

He says to himself, "God will never notice; he covers his face and never sees."

REFLECTION

Yesterday's reading from Psalm 10 was an introduction to the man who has no room for God in his life. The psalmist states, "In his pride the wicked man does not seek him; in all his thoughts there is no room for God" (Psalm 10:4).

Today's reading continues to describe, in disturbing detail, the thoughts, deeds, and attitudes of the heart of such a person. "He says to himself, 'Nothing will ever shake me.' He swears, 'No one will ever do me harm.' His mouth is full of lies and threats; trouble and evil are under his tongue" (Psalm 10:6–7).

Nature abhors a vacuum. All manner of things will rush in to fill an empty space. When God is removed from his rightful place as the master of our life, selfishness and pride rise to the top. If Jesus isn't the Lord of my life, then my selfish nature will rise to the occasion. But when my selfish nature rules, all manner of sin follows. Worst of all, self-deception follows. We deceive ourselves into believing a lie.

The psalmist states, "He says to himself, 'God will never notice; he covers his face and never sees'" (v. 11).

Of course, God does see. Our pride and ignorance are on full display before him. Jesus says this about this topic. "But I tell you that everyone will have to give account on the day of judgment for every empty word they have spoken" (Matthew 12:36).

I have spoken more than a few empty words. How about you? The simple truth is I need a Lord and Master like Jesus to help me govern my life. I also need his love and forgiveness when I slip up.

RESPONSE

Lord Jesus, you are the Lord and Master of the universe. Even the wind and the waves obey you. I want to obey you too. Holy Spirit, blow into my life and fill me with your presence today. Amen.

YOUR TURN

What fills the vacuum in your life? Take some time today to ask Jesus to fill the empty places in your life.

DAY 15: HELPER OF THE FATHERLESS

TODAY'S READING: PSALM 10:12–18

KEY VERSE: PSALM 10:14

But you, God, see the trouble of the afflicted; you consider their grief and take it in hand. The victims commit themselves to you; you are the helper of the fatherless.

REFLECTION

At the start of life there is a father. Without a father there is no life. From the beginning, it has always been so. Ponder those words for a moment.

Those words are also true of a mother as well. But today's psalm focuses on fathers. To be more accurate, the psalmist calls attention to the fatherless. Apparently, fathers aren't just needed at the beginning of life—they are needed throughout life.

There are voices in our society that question the need for fathers. Life, they say, can go on without fathers. In some cases, life is better without them. I would argue that's not life as it should be—as life was designed from the beginning. A huge chunk of the misery, distress, and degradation in this world is caused by the absence of fathers—men who fail to assume their role as fathers. Our prisons are filled with these types of fatherless men.

A good father—an active, involved father—makes a world of difference in the life of a child. As a public school teacher, I saw the truth of this every day. The well-fathered child of either gender has advantages beyond compare on every social, economic, and intellectual scale. We need fathers. And we need one particular father—a perfect Father.

That's why we can draw comfort and encouragement from this psalm. Twice the Lord promises to be a helper and defender of the fatherless. Jesus came to introduce us to our Father—a Father who cares.

RESPONSE

Lord God, father me. Thank you for caring. Help me become the father I need to be. Amen.

YOUR TURN

Has your father made a difference in your life for good or bad? Are you letting God be your Father today?

DAY 16: FAITH UNDER ATTACK

TODAY'S READING: PSALM 11

KEY VERSE: PSALM 11:3

When the foundations are being destroyed, what can the righteous do?

REFLECTION

Do you feel like your faith is under attack? There seem to be people everywhere mocking those who have faith in God. Believers are openly ridiculed. We are blamed for every war since time immemorial. We are told science has rock-solid evidence, while God followers rely on concocted myths handed down by unscrupulous manipulators.

The enemy is firing arrows of accusation, doubt, and distrust "from the shadows at the upright in heart" (Psalm 11:2b). The very foundation of our faith, the Word of God—the Bible—is being attacked as outdated, unreliable, and historically inaccurate. We relate to David when he asked, "When the foundations are being destroyed, what can the righteous do?" (v. 3).

The righteous can do what David does in the first verse of this psalm. David says, "In the LORD I take refuge." For David, God was not a mystical concept. God was a rock-solid reality. David had a memory bank full of experiences with the Lord. The Lord was David's helper, healer, and deliverer. In the tough times of life, God was present in David's life. The Lord brought victory for David over Goliath and over every enemy that exalted itself above God.

The same can be true for you. "Put on the full armor of God, so that you can take your stand against the devil's schemes" (Ephesians 6:11). Remember, "the LORD is on his heavenly throne" (Psalm 11:4b). Nothing takes God by surprise. The Lord is with you and he is watching your response. We need not be intimidated. We need not flee. We need to stand our ground like David and like Paul the Apostle. The Lord is with us.

RESPONSE

Lord, you are my refuge. Help me to stand my ground when my faith is under attack and help other believers to do the same by the grace of Jesus. Amen.

YOUR TURN

Do you have a memory bank full of experiences with the Lord you can draw on? How does reflecting on those past experiences help you now?

DAY 17: WHO CARES FOR THE NEEDY?

TODAY'S READING: PSALM 12

KEY VERSE: PSALM 12:5

"Because the poor are plundered and the needy groan, I will now arise," says the LORD. "I will protect them from those who malign them."

REFLECTION

Who cares for the needy? Certainly not those who constantly strive to get more—more money, a bigger house, more toys. They seem to be far too busy lining their pockets and preparing their golden parachutes to give a thought or a dollar to the poor. The relentless pursuit of profit trumps all other concerns.

Who cares for the poor? Certainly not most political leaders or power brokers. When called upon, they often mouth meaningless platitudes and profess concern. But policy is dictated by those with fat bank accounts and the right connections. They ensure that very little trickles down to those in need. In their hearts, according to verse four of this psalm, they say, "By our tongues we will prevail; our own lips will defend us—who is lord over us?"

Who cares for the poor and needy? According to the words of this psalm, the Lord cares. "'Because the poor are plundered and the needy groan, I will now arise,' says the LORD. 'I will protect them from those who malign them'" (v. 5).

God has always demonstrated concern for the poor. The

prophet Amos declared the Lord's severe judgment on Israel because of their mistreatment of the poor. "For three sins of Israel, even for four, I will not relent. They sell the innocent for silver, and the needy for a pair of sandals. They trample on the heads of the poor as on the dust of the ground and deny justice to the oppressed" (Amos 2:6–7).

Will God judge us for how we treat the poor? Absolutely. God has not changed. He defends the poor and he remains true to his word. The word of the Lord is tried, tested, and true. You can count on it.

RESPONSE

Lord God, give me a caring heart for those who are poor and oppressed. Help me to demonstrate care not just in thought but in practical ways as Jesus would. Amen.

YOUR TURN

What can you do today for someone who is needy or suffering? Let your actions speak.

LIGHT IN A DARK PLACE

TODAY'S READING: PSALM 13

KEY VERSE: PSALM 13:3B–4

Give light to my eyes, or I will sleep in death,
and my enemy will say, "I have overcome him,"
and my foes will rejoice when I fall.

REFLECTION

Have you hit a low point in your life? Are you facing a personal downturn where nothing seems to go right? Problems may arise whether in your career, your finances, your family, or your relations with others. Often difficulty in one area leads to difficulty in other aspects of life. Perhaps you feel that circumstances are conspiring to bring you down. Are you caught in a downward spiral?

David begins Psalm 13 in such a state. His life and career appear to be in a death spiral. He pleads with God, "Give light to my eyes, or I will sleep in death, and my enemy will say, 'I have overcome him,' and my foes will rejoice when I fall" (vv. 3–4).

We can learn a lot from David's response to hard times. First, he brought his problems before God. He poured out his frustration, and in desperation, he called out to the Lord for help. He didn't pretend everything was fine, when clearly, they were not. *Call out to God in times of trouble.*

Second, David asked for the light of God to shine into his situation. "Give light to my eyes, or I will sleep in death ..." When we are going through a dark time, we often can't see our way out. Many times, the solution is right in front of our eyes, but we can't see it. We need God to illumine our path. There is a way forward. We need him to show us. Open your eyes to God's solution.

Finally, David trusted in the unfailing love of God. He rejoiced in God's salvation. God is in the rescue business. The solution had yet to arrive, but in advance, David sang his praise to God. David reflected on the goodness of God. The Lord had been kind and faithful in the past. David knew God would show his goodness once again. Trust and praise God in advance.

RESPONSE

Lord God, I am thankful I can call out to you in times of trouble. Show me the way forward. Open my eyes to the help you are providing and will provide. I trust and thank and praise you in advance. Amen.

YOUR TURN

Has God rescued you in difficult times in the past? Trust him to do the same now and in the future.

DAY 19: THE FOOL FOOLS HIMSELF

Today's Reading: Psalm 14

Key Verse: Psalm 14:1

The fool says in his heart, "There is no God."
They are corrupt, their deeds are vile; there is
no one who does good.

REFLECTION

Apparently, atheism is not a modern phenomenon. Three thousand years ago, in David's time, there were people who said in their heart, "There is no God." Atheism has a long and ignoble pedigree. I say ignoble because, as David observes, it is the fool who says, "There is no God."

There is a footnote in my Bible indicating the word translated in this psalm as *fool* denotes someone who is morally deficient. David goes on to describe what is meant by moral deficiency. He uses the words *corrupt* and *vile*. In fact, there is a complete absence of anything good when it comes to this type of person. But this isn't just David's indictment against a few errant atheists. This is the Lord's view of all mankind. "All have turned away, all have become corrupt; there is no one who does good, not even one" (Psalm 14:3). In the New Testament, the apostle Paul quotes from this psalm in his epistle to the Romans as he outlines the depravity of humanity (see Romans 3:10–18).

Is there a link between unbelief and the sinful state of the human soul? Does sin breed unbelief? There is ample biblical and anecdotal evidence that it does. When Adam and Eve sinned, in an instant, they turned from God seekers to God avoiders. Add a little more sin, and the step is a short one from God avoider to God denier.

We deny the existence of God to avoid accountability for our sin. We foolishly assume since we can't see God, he can't see us and our misdeeds. Better yet, why not pretend God doesn't exist? Then we are at liberty to sin as much as we please without fear of God's judgment. That sounds like morally deficient reasoning to me. The fool fools only himself.

Wisdom begins when we open our hearts and minds to God.

RESPONSE

Father, I want to seek you always, especially when I sin. That's when I need you most. You have the remedy for my sin—the blood of Jesus. You forgive me and clean me up. Amen.

YOUR TURN

Does sinful conduct affect or infect your belief system? How does sin cloud our reasoning?

DAY 20: WHERE I LIVE

TODAY'S READING: PSALM 15

KEY VERSE: PSALM 15:1

LORD, who may dwell in your sacred tent? Who may live on your holy mountain?

REFLECTION

Where are you living? Please note, I did not ask, "What is your address?"

For the Old Testament believer, God had an address. He lived in the Tent of Meeting on Mount Zion in Jerusalem. Later this was the location of the great temple built by Solomon. But this entire psalm is based on the premise that we can live in the presence of God. Why else would David ask, "LORD, who may dwell in your sacred tent? Who may live on your holy mountain?"

Wherever we are, it is possible to live one's life in the conscious presence of the Lord. What an awesome privilege. But how is that possible? On an intellectual level, this is a no brainer. God is present everywhere. We are continually living our lives in full view of an omnipresent God.

Am I always aware of his presence? No, not always.

What can I do to change that? The psalmist lists some requirements for living in the Lord's presence. Apparently, God is vitally concerned with the way we walk out our life of faith—the words we speak, and our interactions with neighbors and friends. The list of requirements found in this psalm is all about practical day-to-day living, being true to our word, loving our neighbor, and being generous to those in need.

The day is coming when I will meet the Lord face to face, but can I see him before that final day? Do I see him in the face of my neighbor?

RESPONSE

Heavenly Father, I don't want to come for an occasional visit. I want to live in your presence now and in eternity. Today, help me interact with others with the knowledge you are watching every thought, word, and action. I'm living with you. Amen.

YOUR TURN

When are you most conscious of God's presence in your life?

DAY 21: EATING AND DRINKING IN GOD

TODAY'S READING: PSALM 16

KEY VERSE: PSALM 16:5

LORD, you alone are my portion and my cup; you
make my lot secure.

REFLECTION

In seed form, all the great truths of the New Testament
are rooted in the Psalms. Psalm 16 perfectly illustrates
this little-known fact. At the start of this psalm, David
declares, "You are my Lord; apart from you I have no
good thing" (Psalm 16:2).

In his epistle to the Romans, Paul writes, "For I know
that good itself does not dwell in me, that is, in my
sinful nature. For I have the desire to do what is good,
but I cannot carry it out" (Romans 7:18). His words are a
rough paraphrase of David's opening thoughts in Psalm
16. All of Romans 7 reflects our great need for our God
and Savior. Without Jesus, there is no redemption and no
hope for victory over sin. But with Paul, we can joyfully
conclude, "Thanks be to God, who delivers me through
Jesus Christ our Lord!" (Romans 7:25).

We find ourselves in full agreement with David's words,
"LORD, you alone are my portion and my cup; you make my
lot secure" (Psalm 16:5). Our Savior is our portion and cup—
our food and drink. He alone is our cup of salvation. Unless
we eat and drink of him, we die. David eloquently expresses
his communion with the Lord. David ate and drank in the

Lord, and so must we. In seed form, David grasped the New Testament concept of communion.

Jesus echoed David's thoughts when he said, "Very truly I tell you, unless you eat the flesh of the Son of Man and drink his blood, you have no life in you. Whoever eats my flesh and drinks my blood has eternal life, and I will raise them up at the last day" (John 6:53–54).

RESPONSE

Heavenly Father, I want to live my life in constant communion with you. I want to live in your presence and eat and drink of you, Lord Jesus. I know "apart from you I have no good thing." And "you are my portion and my cup." I give you thanks. Amen.

YOUR TURN

How are you eating and drinking in God today? How does that concept become a reality?

DAY 22: HEART EXAMS

TODAY'S READING: PSALM 17:1–9

KEY VERSE: PSALM 17:4

Though you probe my heart, though you examine me at night and test me, you will find that I have planned no evil; my mouth has not transgressed.

REFLECTION

"Are you up for the test? The exam schedule has been posted. Have you prepared? Are you ready for it?" Words like those can produce feelings of dread or anxious thoughts, especially for high school or university students. If you have studied and prepared yourself well, you can have a measure of confidence, but some uncertainty always remains.

In verse three of today's psalm, David welcomes God's examination. He states, "Though you probe my heart, though you examine me at night and test me, you will find that I have planned no evil; my mouth has not transgressed."

David had nothing to hide. His conscience was clear. Therefore, he did not dread God's probing. He knew that an examination of his heart would result in vindication. He would be proven right and just before his Maker. Do you and I have the same confidence?

Check your heart. Better yet, allow God to check it regularly. Be open and transparent before him. Doing so is the only way I know to keep a clean heart and a right mind before God and others. The Lord is the best heart doctor available, and he does home visits if we invite him in.

Only when our hearts and minds are open and right before God can we freely pray, "Keep me as the apple of your eye; hide me in the shadow of your wings" (Psalm 17:8).

RESPONSE

Heavenly Father, probe my heart so that I can repent of anything that displeases you. I want to bring only joy and pleasure to the heart of my Father. Amen.

YOUR TURN

Why do we resist allowing God to examine our heart issues? Are we afraid of what he may find?

DAY 23: GOD'S COUNTERATTACK

TODAY'S READING: PSALM 17:10–15

KEY VERSE: PSALM 17:15

As for me, I will be vindicated and will see your face; when I awake, I will be satisfied with seeing your likeness.

REFLECTION

In this world there are those who have a callous heart—a heart that is indifferent to our pain and the suffering of others. Here in Psalm 17, David finds himself surrounded by such people—people who were ready and willing to tear him down. This is a very difficult place to find yourself. This is why David cries out to the Lord for vindication. Earlier in the psalm, he pleads, "Let my vindication come from you; may your eyes see what is right" (Psalm 17:2).

David's response in this very trying situation is highly instructive. He does not try to defend himself. He does not plan a personal counterattack. He has no personal plan for revenge. What tactic does he use? He calls out to the Lord, "Rise up, LORD, confront them, bring them down; with your sword rescue me from the wicked" (Psalm 17:13).

David, the mighty warrior, refuses to use his own sword. Instead, he calls on the Lord to draw his sword and rise to his defense. That takes a lot of faith and a lot of trust in God. When surrounded and attacked, my natural response is to rise in hostile indignation. I'm inclined to counterattack with all guns blazing. But David held his peace. He did not rely on his abilities. He fled to God. He laid out his complaint and asked God to intervene. When King Saul maliciously attacked him, David did not seek revenge. He allowed the Lord to take up his cause and deal with Saul (see 1 Samuel 26).

David's confidence was fully in the Lord. As he concludes this psalm, he declares his confidence with these words: "As for me, I will be vindicated and will see your face; when I awake, I will be satisfied with seeing your likeness" (v. 15).

How confident are you in God's saving intervention on your behalf?

RESPONSE

Heavenly Father, help me to seek vindication from you. Help me put my troubles in your hands. Rise up and come to my defense. Today, I trust in you to act on my behalf. Amen.

YOUR TURN

Do you seek revenge when others have hurt you? Have you asked God to intervene?

DAY 24: MY ROCK

TODAY'S READING: PSALM 18:1–5

KEY VERSE: PSALM 18:3

I called to the LORD, who is worthy of praise, and
I have been saved from my enemies.

REFLECTION

Psalm 18 is one of the longer psalms in the Bible. Step by
step, day by day, we will glean wisdom from the psalmist,
David, as we make our way through this psalm.

In many respects, Psalm 18 is a psalm of culmination.
The introductory note tells us David composed and sang
this psalm, "when the LORD delivered him from the hand
of all his enemies and from the hand of Saul." For many
long years, David had fled for his life from his master King
Saul. At long last, after repeatedly calling on God in great
distress, David has triumphed. And now through the words
of this psalm, he gives all the credit and all the glory to God.

Notice the list of attributes David ascribes to the Lord: my
strength, my rock, my fortress, my deliverer, my God, my rock,
my shield, my salvation, and my stronghold. For David, the
Lord had proven himself repeatedly during years of hard times
to be the embodiment of each of those attributes. If you call on
him, the Lord can be all those things for you as well.

Did you notice that "my rock" is the only attribute that
is repeated in this list? Why do you think David repeated
that phrase? In the prophetic realm, during all those years
of severe testing, Christ was the rock on which David took

his stand. David did not build his life on the shifting sands of public opinion or popularity. He built his life on Christ. A thousand years in advance, David put into practice the words of Jesus, "Therefore everyone who hears these words of mine and puts them into practice is like a wise man who built his house on the rock. The rain came down, the streams rose, and the winds blew and beat against that house; yet it did not fall, because it had its foundation on the rock" (Matthew 7:24–25).

Now that's applied wisdom for the ages.

RESPONSE

Heavenly Father, help me daily to build my life on the rock, Christ Jesus. Lord Jesus, you are my fortress, my salvation, and my stronghold. I put my full trust in you. Amen.

YOUR TURN

How is God like a rock in your life? Has he sustained you during difficult times? Is he helping you through tough times right now, or has he already turned the tide in your favor?

DAY 25: THE LORD THUNDERED FROM HEAVEN

TODAY'S READING: PSALM 18:6–15

KEY VERSES: PSALM 18:13–14

The LORD thundered from heaven; the voice of the Most High resounded. He shot his arrows and scattered the enemy, with great bolts of lightning he routed them.

REFLECTION

Maybe you are like me. I love thunderstorms. But watching a thunderstorm in a city is like watching a Christmas light display in broad daylight. There's something missing. There's no sense of broad expanse or sweeping grandeur.

I grew up on the prairies, and for sheer awe, there's nothing quite like viewing a thunderstorm slowly building in the western sky. Imagine yourself on a slow-moving tractor working a field. Miles of flat land and sky stretch out before you. And the most active thing is the sky. Sometimes the storm clouds hang there boiling and brooding for hours—lightning flashing in the distance. Then suddenly the air changes, the wind picks up, and look out! Lightning! Thunder! Fierce gusts of wind. Rain. Hail. It all comes at you with a vengeance.

I love a thunderstorm because it puts me in my place. The wind, rain, thunder, and lightning highlight who I am. I am a small man in a big world—a world I can control no more than I can control a storm. I'm a man at the mercy of

God. I'm always at the mercy of God whether I see the storm clouds building or not.

In this psalm, David pictures the Lord riding the wings of the wind and thundering from heaven. Not to harm him, but storming in to rescue him in response to his cry for help. That's my God. That's the picture of God I need etched onto my mind. He is the God who hears and answers—the God who helps in times of need. In a vast world, he hears the cry of little, insignificant me. I love a thunderstorm because it shows me the Lord's love and grace.

RESPONSE

Heavenly Father, may I always see you as my helper. Ride to my rescue when times are tough, and I am in need. You are my help and defender. You are worthy of my praise. Amen.

YOUR TURN

Do the storms of life help you see God at work around you?

DAY 26: CLEAN HANDS

TODAY'S READING: PSALM 18:16–24

KEY VERSE: PSALM 18:24

The LORD has rewarded me according to my righteousness, according to the cleanness of my hands in his sight.

REFLECTION

In the previous reading, David depicted the Lord as riding the wings of the wind on a thunderstorm to rescue him from his enemies. In this portion of Psalm 18, the enemy is routed, and David is rescued. In triumph, David declares, "They confronted me in the day of my disaster, but the LORD was my support. He brought me out into a spacious place; he rescued me because he delighted in me" (Psalm 18:18–19).

David then goes on to assert the reason why he believes the Lord did not allow him to perish at the hands of his mortal enemies. Twice he makes this claim, "The LORD has rewarded me according to my righteousness, according to the cleanness of my hands in his sight" (vv. 20, 24).

Why were clean hands so important in David's ultimate victory? Why are clean hands so important to the Lord? Twice when David had the opportunity to cut down his enemies—the enemies who were in pursuit to kill him—David kept his hands clean. When the opportunity arose, David refused to kill jealous King Saul despite the urging of the men who were with him. He attempted reconciliation with the enemy who sought his life (see 1 Samuel 24). That takes courage and conviction.

Sometimes, holding your fire rather than pressing your advantage takes more courage. Abstaining from retaliation takes a godly conviction that God is keeping score, and he will reward the man with a clean heart and clean hands. That takes faith—faith in the unseen hand of God at work in the affairs of men. David had that kind of faith.

How about you? Are your hands clean? Are you trusting in the Lord or settling accounts your way? Faith in God calls us to a higher standard.

RESPONSE

Lord, I want clean hands and a pure heart before you. I put my trust in you. You reward those who diligently seek you. Jesus, wash me clean. I put my faith in you. Amen.

YOUR TURN

Does God always reward those with clean hands? How do you keep your hands clean?

DAY 27: HOW DO YOU SEE GOD?

TODAY'S READING: PSALM 18:25–29

KEY VERSES: PSALM 18:25–26

To the faithful you show yourself faithful, to the blameless you show yourself blameless, to the pure you show yourself pure, but to the devious you show yourself shrewd.

REFLECTION

How do you see God? How do you perceive him? The opening lines of today's psalm tell us plainly the state of our heart determines our perception of God. God reveals himself to us according to the condition of our soul. Therefore, David makes this observation: "To the faithful you show yourself faithful, to the blameless you show yourself blameless, to the pure you show yourself pure, but to the devious you show yourself shrewd."

The truth expressed in this straightforward observation has enormous implications for every human on the planet. Our relationship with God is shaped by our perception of him, and our perception of him is reflective of the state of our heart. For example, one person experiences a period of hardship and loss and turns bitter and angry toward others and God. Another person goes through a similar period of hardship and loss but emerges passionately in love with his creator. How can this be?

The answer can be found in David's observation. "To

the faithful you show yourself faithful, to the blameless you show yourself blameless, to the pure you show yourself pure, but to the devious you show yourself shrewd." The blameless assign no blame to God, but the sin-darkened soul blames him for even the slightest adversity.

Jesus said, "Blessed are the pure in heart, for they will see God" (Matthew 5:8). Do you want to see God at work in your life? Then ask the Lord Jesus to give you a pure heart. God shows himself—becomes visible—to those with a pure heart. The pure in heart see God in the glory of the sunset, in the face of a child, in the kindness of a stranger. The sin-polluted soul can view the same scene—experience the same events—and sees God in none of it. He is blind to God.

Our eyes open the moment we humble ourselves before God. David's words ring true today. "You save the humble but bring low those whose eyes are haughty. You, LORD, keep my lamp burning; my God turns my darkness into light" (Psalm 18:27–29).

RESPONSE

Heavenly Father, give me a pure heart. I want to see you, Lord Jesus, alive and active all around me today. Give me eyes that see beyond the natural and into the realm of the spirit where you are at work. Amen.

YOUR TURN

Did you see God today? How did he show himself to you?

DAY 28: THE WARRIOR'S ARMOR: THE WARRIOR'S STRENGTH

TODAY'S READING: PSALM 18:30–36

KEY VERSE: PSALM 18:34

He trains my hands for battle; my arms can bend a bow of bronze.

REFLECTION

There's a principle of biblical interpretation that goes something like this: The natural comes first, and then comes the spiritual. We can see this illustrated in Paul's comparison of the first man, Adam, with the new man, Christ, in 1 Corinthians 15. Similarly, the natural kingdom of Israel is replaced in the New Testament by the spiritual kingdom of God, which has no physical or geographic boundaries.

In David's time, natural Israel had borders which needed to be defended from attack by flesh and blood enemies that were only too eager to take advantage of any perceived weakness. In the same way today, the church and every born-again believer must be on guard because Satan and his demons are lying in wait, ready to attack.

Yes, Virginia, there is a devil. And he has marked you as his target. He has spiritual murder as his top priority—your murder. "Your enemy the devil prowls around like a roaring lion looking for someone to devour" (1 Peter 5:8).

But God did not leave David or natural Israel defenseless. The Lord provided his matchless word and his impenetrable shield of faith against the foe's attack. Furthermore, there was strength for the battle. David declares, "It is God who arms me with strength and keeps my way secure" (Psalm 18:32). And "He trains my hands for battle; my arms can bend a bow of bronze" (v. 34).

This portion of Psalm 18 has its New Testament spiritual counterpart in Ephesians 6:10–17, where Paul the Apostle, calls us as spiritual warriors to put on the armor of God. Like David, we are in a battle.

RESPONSE

Heavenly Father, help me to fight the good fight. Today, I put on the armor of God to fight the attacks of the enemy. Give me your strength in Christ's name. Amen.

YOUR TURN

How does Satan try to bring you down? What weapons are you using?

DAY 29: THE TRIUMPHANT WARRIOR

TODAY'S READING: PSALM 18:37-45

KEY VERSE: PSALM 18:39

You armed me with strength for battle; you humbled my adversaries before me.

REFLECTION

Do you enjoy sports? Why do you take pride in seeing your home team win? The answer is quite simple: Inside you beats the heart of a warrior. I can deny I have a warrior spirit, but there's a competitive, fighting spirit written into my DNA. It's in your DNA too. In fact, that warrior spirit is essential to your success and survival.

David had an abundant supply of testosterone-fueled warrior spirit, and in the verse above, we see it on full display. Every competitive warrior, like David, signals his triumph. You do as well. This Psalm was part of David's victory celebration.

For a scientific discussion of human response in moments of victory check out the *Time* article "Take That! Athletes' Victory Stances Are All About Dominance, Not Pride."

As a follower of Jesus, the question is not do I have a warrior spirit. The question is how will I direct that warrior's heart into a path that is pleasing to my heavenly Father?

Filled with the Holy Spirit, the twelve disciples turned the world upside down. Their response to Satan's attacks was not merely defensive. Through prayer and proclamation, they took souls captive to the obedience of Christ. The apostle Paul declares, "But thanks be to God, who always leads us as captives in Christ's triumphal procession and uses us to spread the aroma of the knowledge of him everywhere" (2 Corinthians 2:14). Paul was a triumphant warrior in the spiritual realm. David was triumphant in the natural realm. What about you?

RESPONSE

Heavenly Father, help me rise up as a spiritual warrior for you today. Help me *to spread the aroma of the knowledge of* Jesus everywhere. Through the power of Christ, I know I am more than a conqueror. Amen.

YOUR TURN

Are you personally gaining ground in the spiritual battle all around you?

DAY 30: THE LIVING ROCK

TODAY'S READING: PSALM 18:46–50

KEY VERSE: PSALM 18:46

The LORD lives! Praise be to my Rock! Exalted
be God my Savior!

REFLECTION

The joyful exuberance of the opening lines of this final
reading from Psalm 18 is well worth reflecting upon. David
exults, "The LORD lives! Praise be to my Rock! Exalted be
God my Savior!"

To my thinking, there's nothing quite as dead as a rock.
But in the same breath, David praises the living Lord, his
rock and Savior. Living rock seems to be a contradiction in
terms, but our God is very much alive. He was alive and
active in David's life, and he is alive and active in your life
as well—as active and alive as you allow him to be.

But the Lord also wants to be the rock of stability in your
life—the solid foundation from which you draw strength. A
life anchored in God can withstand the storms of adversity
and the test of time. The Lord is that stalwart mainstay that
actively trains us for eternity.

Most importantly, our Lord saves. He saved David
from all his troubles. It was God's intervention in David's
life that brought him the victory time after time. God was
not content to sit in heaven and cheer from the sidelines.

The Lord involved himself in David's life. He responded repeatedly to David's cries for mercy and help.

If David had ample reasons to praise God and be thankful, we who live on this side of the cross, under the new covenant, have far more grounds for praise. God intervened directly for us. We have a savior in Jesus, who left his throne in glory. He put his own skin in the game. The Father sent his one and only Son to live as a man, and then suffer and die on our behalf. And Jesus did not remain dead. God the Father raised him from the dead. Now, with David, we can say, "The LORD lives! Praise be to my Rock! Exalted be God my Savior!"

RESPONSE

Heavenly Father, thank you for sending Jesus. Thank you for his life, his death, and his resurrection. I love you, Lord Jesus. You are the living rock on which I can build my life. Through you I am more than a conqueror. Holy Spirit help me live this day in praise of my Savior. Amen.

YOUR TURN

Is the Lord your living rock? Has he been your help? Has Jesus become your Savior? How will you honor him today?

DAY 31: DOES THE SKY TALK TO YOU?

TODAY'S READING: PSALM 19:1–6

KEY VERSE: PSALM 19:1

The heavens declare the glory of God; the skies proclaim the work of his hands.

REFLECTION

When was the last time you went for a walk beneath a canopy of stars? Now, I'm not talking about catching a fleeting glimpse of a dozen or so stars, obscured by the incessant glare of city streetlights. I'm talking about walking beneath a canopy of stars, visible in their myriads, stretching from horizon to horizon. Now that's a truly awe-inspiring experience!

That's where David begins this psalm—beneath the stars. He begins his song beneath a sky so big it reduces any who behold it to a mere speck of insignificance—a speck below the glorious vastness above. Can you see David standing there—the youthful shepherd—on the Judean hillside, gazing into the face of eternity?

And eternity—the sky—is talking to him. What is it saying? Can you hear its words? David can. He hears the heavens pouring forth speech. And it's not just the night sky that's talking to him. The heavens are speaking continually, day and night. This is an endless conversation heard around the world.

You see, the sky speaks in a language understood by all. Who has not stopped and stood in wonder at the sight of a dazzling sunset, marveled at the shafts of light beaming down from behind a thunderhead, or been amazed by the appearance of a rainbow? Perhaps you have seen the aurora whirl and dance across the northern sky.

These experiences are universal. They are available to all, on every continent, in every nation, to every language and people group. The sky is talking. Are you listening? Do you understand the words?

RESPONSE

Heavenly Father, help me hear your voice speaking to me in nature. Open my eyes and my ears to the glory of your creation. You are more wonderful than I can imagine. I praise you for all your marvelous works. Amen.

YOUR TURN

Does God speak to you through the beauty of nature? Have you paused recently to wonder at the majesty of his creation?

DAY 32: THE POWER OF THE WORD REFRESHING THE SOUL

TODAY'S READING: PSALM 19:7–11

KEY VERSE: PSALM 19:7

The law of the LORD is perfect, refreshing the soul. The statutes of the LORD are trustworthy, making wise the simple.

REFLECTION

The voice of the speaking stars (see yesterday's reading) is now joined by the voice of the written Holy Word. If nature, specifically the sky, is the first witness to testify to the glory of God, then the Scriptures—the written word of God—constitute the second great witness to speak of God's existence. Both these great witnesses have gathered here to testify within the context of Psalm 19.

While nature speaks to us of the existence of God the creator, it is largely silent regarding the nature or character of this all-powerful supernatural being. Is he good? Is he evil? Is he indifferent to us? Is he angry with us? What is this great, overarching, omnipresent God really like? May we approach him?

God's word shows us the way. In verse 7, David tells us, "The law of the LORD is perfect, refreshing the soul."

The law is perfect, flawless, inerrant, and infallible. Only a perfect, flawless, inerrant, and infallible God can be the source of such a document. The law of the Lord referred to here is, in fact, the Bible, the Word of God. Jack Hayford, in his commentary on this verse from the Psalms, states, "That the 'law of the Lord is perfect,' is direct reference to the absolute, complete, and entire trustworthiness of the Holy Scriptures, which constitute the Bible."

There is great power in the written word. The word of God is redemptive, personal, and transformational. This perfect, true, and infallible law, or Word of God, has an effect. The Word of God is active and revives the soul. God's word literally brings souls back to spiritual life.

RESPONSE

Lord God, help me draw life, wisdom, and joy from your Word every day. Light my way. Amen.

YOUR TURN

Do you read God's Word daily? How has it helped you grow in faith?

DAY 33: I NEED FORGIVENESS. WHAT ABOUT YOU?

TODAY'S READING: PSALM 19:12–14

KEY VERSE: PSALM 19:12–13A

But who can discern their own errors? Forgive my hidden faults. Keep your servant also from willful sins; may they not rule over me.

REFLECTION

What is your response to God's Word and his voice when it speaks to your heart? In this final portion of Psalm 19, we see David's response to God. God has been doing the talking thus far. The Lord has been speaking to David through the stars, through the night sky, and the blazing heat of the sun—the first witness. He has spoken to him through the Word of God—his written revelation—the second witness. Now, as this psalm draws to a close, we hear David responding back to God.

Actually, David is responding to the third witness. His heart is bearing witness to the reality of God. His conscience is convicting him of his sin and of the righteousness of God. We all have this third witness within us—a witness that will not be silenced, though we may try to drown out this inner voice of the Spirit. The Holy Spirit is always at work when we respond in a right way to God.

If along with David, we have heard the voices of the first and second witness, then there is only one appropriate response. It is the response recorded here in Holy Scriptures. If we see and grasp the awesome power and majesty of God, if through his Word, we have glimpsed his holiness, then we are brought low. We are humbled before him. Our greatest achievements are nothing. Our pride dissolves. Our weakness, our smallness is self-evident in the presence of the Lord of heaven and earth. We are exposed, and our sin is exposed before this holy, magnificent God.

Along with David, we cry out, "But who can discern their own errors? Forgive my hidden faults. Keep your servant also from willful sins; may they not rule over me."

If we perceive God correctly, and if we assess ourselves accurately and honestly, then we quickly realize our greatest need. Our greatest need is for forgiveness. This is the solid bedrock on which any human relationship with God is built.

Here is the truth. I need forgiveness. My failings and shortcomings are many. What about you?

RESPONSE

Heavenly Father, please forgive my sins. Often, I have lived according to my will, not yours. Forgive my selfish ways. "May these words of my mouth and this meditation of my heart be pleasing in your sight, LORD, my Rock and my Redeemer" (Psalm 19:14). Amen.

YOUR TURN

Have you confessed your hidden sins to God? Have you acknowledged your need for a Savior from yourself?

DAY 34: ARE YOU SPEAKING WORDS OF BLESSING?

TODAY'S READING: PSALM 20

KEY VERSE: PSALM 20:4

May he give you the desire of your heart and make all your plans succeed.

REFLECTION

There's an old saying that's attributed to St. Augustine, "Pray as if everything depends on God. Work as if everything depends on you." Here in Psalm 20, in the form of a prayer, David captures the essence of that thought. But David is not praying for himself. He is praying for your success. Hear his words: "May he [the Lord] give you the desire of your heart and make all your plans succeed. May we shout for joy over your victory and lift up our banners in the name of our God. May the LORD grant all your requests" (Psalm 20:4–5 addition mine).

David's prayer on behalf of others brings a measure of conviction to my heart. How much time do I spend praying for the success of others? I tend to be rather selfish in my prayer requests. Do I want personal victories more than corporate or team success? Am I earnest in my desire to see others grow and prosper or is there a root of jealous envy that restricts my prayers on their behalf? Do I speak words of blessing over those around me? Do I inwardly rejoice when my brother stumbles because his failure helps me look successful?

The opening half of this psalm is intended as a spoken blessing over the life of my brother and my friend. Take a moment right now and substitute your friend's name into this psalm wherever the word "you" appears. Now speak the opening lines of this psalm as a blessing over your friend's life. Finally, trust in the Lord your God to work on behalf of your friend or family member. We serve a God who brings victory.

RESPONSE

Heavenly Father, I repent of jealousy and envy. Help me speak words of blessing over those around me. I trust you. You are the true source of health and blessing in this world. Amen.

YOUR TURN

Whose life can you speak God's blessing into today? Are there family members, friends, or colleagues that need the blessing of God?

DAY 35: ARE YOU BEING TESTED BY SUCCESS?

TODAY'S READING: PSALM 21:1–7

KEY VERSE: PSALM 21:1

The king rejoices in your strength, LORD. How great is his joy in the victories you give!

REFLECTION

The greatest test of a man's character does not come during times of failure and defeat, but rather during times of success and victory. The higher a person rises, the more detached he becomes from the common man's reality. The historian Lord Acton observed that "Power tends to corrupt and absolute power corrupts absolutely."

Despite much opposition, conflict, and affliction, David, the shepherd boy, became the king of Israel. David's character was severely tested as he wandered as a fugitive in the wilderness, but greater testing lay ahead. David's moral failure came at the pinnacle of his success. He passed the test in the wilderness but failed the test in the throne room. Nothing tests a man's mettle like success.

Despite this weakness, David knew where his strength lay. His strength came from the Lord. He knew the true source of his success. In verse 1 of Psalm 21, he testifies to why he rose to prominence: "The king rejoices in your strength, LORD. How great is his joy in the victories you give!"

When we achieve success, we need to cast our mind back to the reason for that success. It's interesting to note David did not take the credit for his victories. He attributed his accomplishments to the Lord. This is contrary to human nature. I am apt to crow about my triumphs rather than give the credit to God. The truth is my abilities come from God and any success I achieve comes as a gift from him. "For promotion and power come from nowhere on earth, but only from God. He promotes one and deposes another" (Psalm 75:6–7 TLB).

RESPONSE

Heavenly Father, help me to rightly handle the success you bring. Lord Jesus, you are my victory over death, hell, and the grave. Keep me thankful. You are more wonderful than I can imagine. I praise you. I owe any success I have achieved to you, Lord. Amen.

YOUR TURN

What personal success can you thank God for today? Are you giving credit where credit is due?

DAY 36: DO YOU HAVE THE RIGHT PICTURE OF GOD?

TODAY'S READING: PSALM 21:8–13

KEY VERSE: PSALM 21:9

When you appear for battle, you will burn them up as in a blazing furnace. The LORD will swallow them up in his wrath, and his fire will consume them.

REFLECTION

I have a confession to make. I love the Psalms, but there are some psalms where my fondness runs very thin. That's the case with this one. The pacifist side of me gets very uncomfortable with all this talk of God's wrath burning like a consuming fire. My reasoning goes something like this: If God gets angry with others, I might be the next one to get burned.

In this psalm, David paints a portrait of the Lord as a warrior. I'm not so sure I want to see the Lord as a fearsome warrior. I prefer to see him as a gentle shepherd—the Good Shepherd—not a God of vengeance firing arrows at his foes. But if I have my way—if I see him only as a meek shepherd—do I have a right picture of the Lord? Am I blind to an important side of his character? Is he both a warrior and a shepherd?

I can be guilty of shaping God according to my image— the likeness I prefer. But the god I create is not the true

God. The true God is always greater, more awesome, fear-provoking, and loving than I can possibly imagine. Words on a page fall short when we attempt to describe God.

As for this world, it's inhabited by evil men. Some are heinously evil—monsters in human skin. Others, by the mercy of God, are filled with kindness. A measure of the grace of God is extended even to those who do not know him. If God refused to rain judgment on the perpetrators of evil, would he still be a good God? If this world were perfect, would we still long for heaven?

Who am I to judge God? Who am I to find fault with my Creator and his ways? Here is the conclusion: Ride on in the battle against evil, Warrior King. Shelter me in your arms, Good Shepherd.

RESPONSE

Heavenly Father, I confess I have an incomplete picture of you. I can never grasp or comprehend your fullness. I bow before you, Lord Almighty. In humility, I worship you, the magnificent and perfect, I AM. Amen.

YOUR TURN

Has your picture of God changed over time? Has it become more biblically accurate?

DAY 37: DO YOU BELIEVE IN PROPHECY?

TODAY'S READING: PSALM 22:1–8

KEY VERSE: PSALM 22:1

My God, my God, why have you forsaken me? Why are you so far from saving me, so far from my cries of anguish?

REFLECTION

Do you believe in prophecy?

Psalm 22 is the most graphic description of Christ's crucifixion found anywhere in the Bible. Yet here it is—tucked away among the Psalms—written roughly nine hundred years before the birth of Christ. How can this be? During David's time, crucifixion as a form of execution had not yet been invented. Furthermore, crucifixion is portrayed from the victim's point of view—the point of view of Jesus.

"My God, my God, why have you forsaken me?" These are the words of Jesus on the cross (Matthew 27:46) and they form the opening line of this psalm. Of course, Jesus knew he was quoting this psalm when he cried out in anguish. But did his arrogant mockers know they too were fulfilling scriptural prophecy as they hurled their insults, "He trusts in the LORD," they say, "let the LORD rescue him. Let him deliver him, since he delights in him." These words from verse 8 of Psalm 22 find an uncanny parallel in the verbal abuse thrown at Jesus in Matthew 27:43. "He trusts in God. Let God rescue him now if he wants him, for he said, 'I am the Son of God.'"

Remarkably, David saw everything. Through the inspiration of the Holy Spirit, he beheld the cross nine centuries in advance. I believe in prophecies to come because of prophesies fulfilled.

RESPONSE

Father, thank you for sending your Son Jesus to this cruel world to suffer on my behalf. Thank you that I can put my trust in your Holy Word. It was, is, and will be forever true and trustworthy. Amen.

YOUR TURN

Why do you have confidence in God's Word?

DAY 38: WHAT DOES A SUFFERING SAVIOR MEAN FOR YOU?

TODAY'S READING: PSALM 22:9–15

KEY VERSE: PSALM 22:15

My mouth is dried up like a potsherd, and my tongue sticks to the roof of my mouth; you lay me in the dust of death.

REFLECTION

From a prophetic standpoint, this is a crucifixion psalm. As stated in the previous devotion, in Psalm 22, the crucifixion is portrayed from the victim's point of view— Christ's point of view. Jesus is speaking through the poetic medium of this psalm. He describes his thoughts amid the horror of his excruciating affliction.

I recently read an account of the disastrous Dieppe Raid of 1942. In one scene from the carnage on the Normandy beach, a horribly mangled, mortally wounded young man is trapped in coils of razor wire. Do you know what he does with his last desperate gasps? He cries out for his mother. In the pain of death, the thoughts of grown men often turn to the soothing remembrance of their mother's love. It was no different for our Savior. Jesus put his trust in God from birth. "Yet you brought me out of the womb; you made me trust in you, even at my mother's breast. From birth I was cast on you; from my mother's womb you have been my God" (vv. 9–10).

As Jesus hangs pinned to the cross, he is encircled by his accusers—strong bulls of Bashan—who hurl insults at him. Peering down at his mangled and bleeding body, he laments, "I am poured out like water, and all my bones are out of joint. My heart has turned to wax; it has melted within me" (v. 14).

As the heat of the day builds, the trickle of blood continues and severe dehydration sets in. He cries out, "I thirst!" (John 19:28). This is our Savior's confession—his stark reality—a reality he endured for our redemption. "My mouth is dried up like a potsherd, and my tongue sticks to the roof of my mouth; you lay me in the dust of death" (Psalm 22:15).

What we see portrayed in this psalm is a portrait of love—redeeming love that reaches out to me, a fallen man.

RESPONSE

Father God, thank you for sending your Son Jesus to this cruel world to suffer on my behalf. Your unconditional love for me was demonstrated on the cross for all to see. I thank you. Amen.

YOUR TURN

What does the suffering of Jesus mean for you?

DAY 39: HIS HANDS AND FEET WERE PIERCED FOR ME

TODAY'S READING: PSALM 22:16–21

KEY VERSE: PSALM 22:16

Dogs surround me, a pack of villains encircles me; they pierce my hands and my feet.

REFLECTION

The title notes to Psalm 22 state, "A psalm of David." But while this is David's psalm, it's entirely about Jesus—about our Savior's personal thoughts and experience, about his suffering and death. Nowhere is this expressed more clearly than in the key verse above: "Dogs surround me, a pack of villains encircles me; they pierce my hands and my feet."

On the rock hill called Golgotha, surrounded by his taunting enemies, Jesus is stripped naked. His hands and feet are pierced as he is nailed to the cross and lifted up for the whole world to see. The helpless Christ silently laments, "All my bones are on display; people stare and gloat over me" (v. 17).

All four Gospels record what happens next. The soldiers divide up Christ's clothes and gamble for his seamless garment. "'Let's not tear it,' they said to one another. 'Let's decide by lot who will get it.' This happened that the scripture might be fulfilled that said, 'They divided my clothes among them and cast lots for my garment.' So this is what the soldiers did" (John 19:24).

Thoughtless Roman soldiers fulfilled what David penned nine centuries earlier. But was Jesus truly helpless? If he was helpless, he was helpless by design. If he was forsaken by his Father, he was forsaken by choice—his choice. This was a course of action Jesus willingly chose. He lay down his life. The Lamb of God suffered and died that our sins might be atoned, that we may receive a full pardon. Redemption has come. The price has been paid in full—paid in blood.

The turning point in this psalm is found in the last verse of our reading today. With unvoiced words, Jesus cries out to be rescued and delivered from death. Three days later, his prayer was answered through his bodily resurrection. Ultimately, Jesus triumphed over death, hell, and the grave. By faith, his suffering brings our redemption and victory.

RESPONSE

Lord Jesus, my praise flows to you. You were forsaken that I might have eternal life. Thank you for thinking of me rather than of yourself. You deserve all praise. Amen.

YOUR TURN

What is the right response to the love Jesus showed?

DAY 40: CHRIST'S SUFFERING AND OUR SUFFERING

TODAY'S READING: PSALM 22:22–26

KEY VERSE: PSALM 22:24

For he has not despised or scorned the suffering of the afflicted one; he has not hidden his face from him but has listened to his cry for help.

REFLECTION

In this ongoing discussion of Psalm 22, we hit a critical turning point with yesterday's Scripture reading. The humiliated, pierced, and tortured Christ prays, "But you, LORD, do not be far from me. You are my strength; come quickly to help me. Deliver me from the sword, my precious life from the power of the dogs. Rescue me from the mouth of the lions; save me from the horns of the wild oxen" (vv. 19–21).

God the Father answered the prayer of his suffering Son, not immediately, but three days later when Jesus arose from the dead. Now, he reigns triumphant over death, hell, and the grave. The opening words of today's reading are Christ's resurrected song of triumph: "I will declare your name to my people; in the assembly I will praise you. You who fear the LORD, praise him! All you descendants of Jacob, honor him! Revere him, all you descendants of Israel!" (vv. 22–23)

And why should we praise the Lord? The answer is found in verse 24: "For he has not despised or scorned the suffering of the afflicted one; he has not hidden his face from him but has listened to his cry for help."

In the context of this psalm, Christ is the afflicted one. The prophet Isaiah declares, "He was pierced for our transgressions, he was crushed for our iniquities; the punishment that brought us peace was on him, and by his wounds we are healed" (Isaiah 53:5).

Yes, praise him! We have a Savior who can fully identify with every aspect of our humanity because he was fully human. He suffered just as we suffer and, in his body, he experienced severe loss and pain. God incarnate knows all about the human condition because he lived as a human. But in all this Jesus is the victor. "May your hearts live forever" (Psalm 22:26), because of Jesus Christ, who conquered death and lives now and forever.

RESPONSE

Father, thank you for victory over death, hell, and the grave through your Son Jesus. By faith, his victory becomes my victory. Hallelujah! I praise you my Lord and Savior. Amen.

YOUR TURN

Does the knowledge of Christ's suffering help you in times of personal pain or loss?

DAY 41: THE ENDS OF THE EARTH TURN TO THE LORD

TODAY'S READING: PSALM 22:27–31

KEY VERSES: PSALM 22:27–28

All the ends of the earth will remember and turn to the LORD, and all the families of the nations will bow down before him, for dominion belongs to the LORD and he rules over the nations.

REFLECTION

This final portion of Psalm 22 signals the ultimate triumph of the Lord Jesus Christ. In the first half of this psalm, Christ's humiliation, suffering, and death by crucifixion are vividly portrayed. With stunning accuracy and detail, David depicts these events from Christ's perspective. Only God-breathed prophetic insight could reveal such truth through a human vessel. "For prophecy never had its origin in the human will, but prophets, though human, spoke from God as they were carried along by the Holy Spirit" (2 Peter 1:21).

With today's reading, we discover the worldwide impact of Christ's redemptive death and resurrection. "All the ends of the earth will remember and turn to the LORD, and all the families of the nations will bow down before him, for dominion belongs to the LORD and he rules over the nations" (Psalm 22:27–28).

Christ's gospel—the good news of the kingdom—has been voiced abroad. Death, hell, and the grave have been conquered. Jesus Christ is Lord over all! Keep in mind that this turning to the Lord by "all the families of the nations" was an alien concept to the people of Israel during David's time. Yet again, David spoke prophetically of the time when the gospel message would burst forth from its Jewish cocoon and be declared and received by ready hearts all over the world. Our Savior's commission will be fulfilled. "Therefore go and make disciples of all nations, baptizing them in the name of the Father and of the Son and of the Holy Spirit, and teaching them to obey everything I have commanded you. And surely I am with you always, to the very end of the age" (Matthew 28:19–20).

Psalm 22 concludes with the promise of the worldwide spread of the gospel from generation to generation. "Posterity will serve him; future generations will be told about the LORD. They will proclaim his righteousness, declaring to a people yet unborn: He has done it!" (vv. 30–31)

RESPONSE

Father, thank you for the good news of the gospel. Jesus is alive and reigns forever. Help me to do my part in bringing the message of your love and redemption to the world. I want to see people from all nations turning to you in repentance and faith. Amen.

YOUR TURN

How can we spread the good news? What are you doing to tell his story?

DAY 42: ARE YOU PURSUING THE GOOD LIFE?

TODAY'S READING: PSALM 23

KEY VERSE: PSALM 23:1

The LORD is my shepherd, I lack nothing.

REFLECTION

If there is a biblical recipe or prescription for the good life, it can be found in the words of this psalm. This is a psalm that drips with satisfaction. It oozes with the very fullness of life and overflows with a quiet peace. There is a mellow ripeness to these words that runs down your chin, lights a spark in your eye, and puts a spring in your step.

We live in a world that is in feverish pursuit of the good life. The self-centered pursuit of happiness has become the crowning, but ever elusive goal. That word "pursuit" says it all. Apparently, we should chase after happiness. But can happiness be found in a host of products, devices, and programs?

A profoundly different model for the good life is found within the words of this psalm. The good life, which in our hearts we all seek, is anchored in the Good Shepherd. Jesus is that Good Shepherd. Listen to his words, "I am the good shepherd; I know my sheep, and my sheep know me" (John 10:14). Is the Lord your shepherd? If he is, then all the rest follows: refreshment, goodness, and love simply trail along behind him as you follow in his steps. The beauty of following the Good Shepherd is so obvious, you can miss it, because it seems far too simple.

In following him, rather than following our own desires, happiness comes. There is an abundance that comes into play the moment we surrender our stubborn will to the Good Shepherd and then begin to follow him with our whole heart.

RESPONSE

O Lord my God, I want to follow you. Dear Jesus, be my Good Shepherd, now and throughout this life you have given me. I love you because you first loved me. I want the good life that comes from following you. Amen.

YOUR TURN

Why do self-centered pursuits leave us feeling empty?

DAY 43: THE GENERATION THAT SEEKS GOD

TODAY'S READING: PSALM 24:1–6

KEY VERSE: PSALM 24:3

Who may ascend the mountain of the LORD? Who may stand in his holy place?

REFLECTION

Psalm 24 begins by establishing the sovereignty of the Lord. He alone is to be worshiped because the Lord is the Creator of all things. "The earth is the LORD's, and everything in it, the world, and all who live in it; for he founded it on the seas and established it on the waters" (vv. 1–2).

David goes on to ask two very pertinent questions. "Who may ascend the mountain of the LORD? Who may stand in his holy place?" (v. 3).

Can anyone approach this great Sovereign God? Are there any preconditions that we need to meet? According to David, the answer is yes. "The one who has clean hands and a pure heart, who does not trust in an idol or swear by a false god" (v. 4).

David, I have a problem with that answer. You see my hands aren't always clean, and my heart isn't always pure. How then can I approach the Lord? In fact, my problem is a universal problem. In Psalm 14:2–3, we read this indictment against humanity: "The LORD looks down from heaven on all mankind to see if there are any who understand, any who seek God. All have turned away, all have become corrupt; there is no one who does good, not even one."

Is this generation seeking the Lord? With rare exceptions, the answer is no. It has always been thus. The harsh words of Psalm 24 ring just as true now as they did in David's time. But there are those who break the mold of this world—those who have received the forgiveness and cleansing of God. "They will receive blessing from the LORD and vindication from God their Savior. Such is the generation of those who seek him, who seek your face, God of Jacob" (vv. 5–6).

Those who have been cleansed by the blood of the Lamb of God may freely approach the throne of God. I want to be numbered among that generation.

RESPONSE

Lord Jesus, I thank you for your suffering and death on the cross. Your blood cleanses my hands and purifies my heart. Today I want to seek you. In your great mercy reveal yourself to me. Amen.

YOUR TURN

Are you a God seeker? On what basis do you approach the Sovereign Lord?

DAY 44: WELCOME THE KING OF GLORY

TODAY'S READING: PSALM 24:7–10

KEY VERSE: PSALM 24:7

Lift up your heads, you gates; be lifted up, you ancient doors, that the King of glory may come in.

REFLECTION

Are you ready? The King is coming.

All of Psalm 24 is a psalm of anticipation. David, the shepherd king, is anticipating the arrival of the Lord. The Lord is coming to his city—to his temple. Have you prepared your heart and your mind for the moment of his arrival? Are you ready to receive him as your king? He often shows up at the moment we least expect him.

Undoubtedly, David, the warrior king, reflected on his own triumphant entry into the city after the defeat of his enemies in battle. But here in this psalm, he projects the victorious arrival of a much greater monarch—the King of Glory.

There is a prophetic expectancy to this psalm that forms a very natural bridge to the Palm Sunday triumphal entry of Jesus into Jerusalem. Jesus, the long-anticipated King, came suddenly to his temple. Some were ready for him, but most were not. The fact that we could miss his appearing should infuse our preparations for the King with an element of urgency.

Earlier in this psalm, David asks, "Who may stand in his

holy place?" (v. 3). Purity of heart and action are essential. Blessing and vindication await those who seek his face. Again, I ask, "Are you ready?" God can show up in your life today in an unexpected way. Will you recognize him? Or, like the busy people of Jerusalem, will that moment pass you by? Will you be too caught up in buying and selling and the commerce of our times? Will you be too distracted by social media to recognize the medium of the Holy Spirit?

Lift up your head. Open your eyes. Take your attention off the mundane things of this world and focus the eyes of your heart on the Lord. Seek his face in your daily routine. The King of Glory may be passing by today.

RESPONSE

Come, Lord Jesus, come. I open my heart and my mind to you. I want to see you at work in my daily circumstances. King of Glory, help me to anticipate your appearing in my life today. Grant me a pure heart so I can recognize your coming. Amen.

YOUR TURN

Has the King of Glory appeared in your life recently? What are you doing to prepare for him?

DAY 45: HOW CAN I AVOID BEING PUT TO SHAME?

TODAY'S READING: PSALM 25:1–7

KEY VERSE: PSALM 25:2

I trust in you; do not let me be put to shame,
nor let my enemies triumph over me.

REFLECTION

Shame is a very negative feeling. Some pop psychologists believe this emotional response should be completely removed from our lives. They argue shame has no useful function since it often holds us back from exploring and experimenting with new behaviors and activities in the world around us.

A life lived without any sense of shame, is life without an active conscience. Those who lack a shame gland soon find themselves trapped in self-destructive behavior that spirals out of control. A sense of shame when we have done wrong can act as the messenger of God calling us to repentance and a change of heart.

Here in this psalm, David pleads with the Lord that he will not be put to shame. That should be our prayer as well. And how can we avoid being put to shame? In verse 3, David gives us the answer. "No one who hopes in you will ever be put to shame, but shame will come on those who are treacherous without cause."

If your hope is in the Lord, he will protect you from shame and disgrace. Trusting in God, rather than in ourselves, is the point where freedom from shame begins. A humble, teachable spirit is what God desires. Because of his great mercy and love, he forgives the sins of our youth and our rebellious ways. Praise the Lord!

RESPONSE

Lord, this is my prayer: "Show me your ways, LORD, teach me your paths. Guide me in your truth and teach me, for you are God my Savior, and my hope is in you all day long" (vv. 4–5). Amen.

YOUR TURN

How does trusting in God protect you from experiencing shame?

DAY 46: DO YOU SEEK GUIDANCE FOR YOUR LIFE?

TODAY'S READING: PSALM 25:8–15

KEY VERSE: PSALM 25:8

Good and upright is the LORD; therefore he instructs sinners in his ways.

REFLECTION

Some truths are self-evident: Water flows downhill, always has and always will. Darkness is an absence of light. The first line of today's psalm reading is also one of those self-evident truths. "Good and upright is the LORD." The Lord is always good, and he is always upright in all his ways. There is nothing devious or corrupt about him. That's simply the nature of our God.

Because the Lord is good and upright, righteousness and grace flow from his throne. The Lord "instructs sinners in his ways. He guides the humble in what is right and teaches them his way" (vv. 8–9). His love cascades down upon those who are humble of heart. Jesus, in his earthly ministry, exemplified the very nature of God, because he came as the Lord in human flesh. He said, "Come to me, all you who are weary and burdened, and I will give you rest. Take my yoke upon you and learn from me, for I am gentle and humble in heart, and you will find rest for your souls" (Matthew 11:28–29).

Are you learning from Jesus? Have you positioned

yourself to hear and follow him? The Lord is our teacher, but he only instructs those who humbly fear and reverence him. The obstinate sinner has shut his ears to the voice of God. There is no guidance from heaven for him, nor does he seek direction, because in rebellion he has chosen his own path.

Do you want the Lord to guide you in the decisions you face? Be of good cheer. If you fear the Lord, he will instruct you in the way you should choose. Confess your sin to him, admit your need before him, and then open your spirit to hear from God. We have this promise, "The LORD confides in those who fear him" (Psalm 25:14).

RESPONSE

Lord, in humility I come before you. I need your help and guidance every moment of the day. Teach me your ways in every situation and circumstance that I face. Amen.

YOUR TURN

Do you routinely ask for the Lord's guidance? How has he responded? Can you testify to situations in which the Lord has guided your steps?

DAY 47: DAVID: BRAVE HEART OR LONELY HEART

TODAY'S READING: PSALM 25:16–22

KEY VERSE: PSALM 25:16

Turn to me and be gracious to me, for I am lonely and afflicted.

REFLECTION

David begins Psalm 25 on a note of confidence, but as this psalm draws to a close, he truly bears his heart. David plaintively calls out to the Lord, "Turn to me and be gracious to me, for I am lonely and afflicted."

The warrior king lets his guard down and we see into his soul. There is a time for putting on a brave face, and there's a time for open and transparent honesty. Here within the context of this psalm, we see both. David, the brave heart and David, the lonely heart. Earlier in the psalm, David showed absolute confidence in his God, but now he pours out his soul in humble petition. Hear the cry of his heart, "Relieve the troubles of my heart and free me from my anguish. Look on my affliction and my distress and take away all my sins" (vv. 17–18).

David recognized his greatest need—forgiveness. That's our greatest need too. We need the peace of mind that forgiveness brings.

David was surrounded by mortal enemies, and so are we. The legions of hell are arrayed against the Christian believer. At this moment, worldly philosophies and demonic forces are conspiring to destroy your home, your marriage, and your life. Along with David we pray, "See how numerous are my enemies and how fiercely they hate me! Guard my life and rescue me; do not let me be put to shame, for I take refuge in you" (vv. 19–20).

Our hope must always be centered in the Lord. Integrity and uprightness form a wall of protection around the people of God. But our deliverance comes from the Lord. Along with David we affirm, "No one who hopes in you will ever be put to shame" (v. 3).

RESPONSE

Lord Jesus, help me to be open and transparent before you. Take away all my sins. My hope is in you. Protect me the attacks of the enemy. Deliver me from all my troubles. Amen.

YOUR TURN

How much do you need God? Do you need his forgiveness? What spiritual enemies are you facing?

DAY 48: ARE YOU READY TO BE TESTED?

TODAY'S READING: PSALM 26:1–7

KEY VERSES: PSALM 26:2–3

Test me, LORD, and try me, examine my heart and my mind; for I have always been mindful of your unfailing love and have lived in reliance on your faithfulness.

REFLECTION

The opening lines of Psalm 26 certainly catch my attention. David claims to have led a blameless life—a rather audacious statement, in my opinion. But he doesn't stop there. He goes on to invite God to test him. David pleads, "Test me, LORD, and try me, examine my heart and my mind; for I have always been mindful of your unfailing love and have lived in reliance on your faithfulness."

Now that takes some nerve. Do I really want the Lord to examine my heart and my mind? If I underwent a heart and mind exam, what would my test scores be? Most of us would shy away from being tested by God, but David's response is completely different. He is clearly saying, "Bring it on!"

How could David be so self-assured—so confident—to the point of sounding arrogant? Actually, David's confidence was not so much in his own performance, but rather, his confidence is in God. He states he is mindful of the Lord's unfailing love. He relies on the Lord's faithfulness. David knew the unfailing love and faithfulness of God, and this wasn't merely head knowledge—a bit of mental information.

No. David knew God experientially. He experienced the Lord's unfailing love and faithfulness over and over in his life. As a youth, he slew a marauding lion and a bear. He brought down the mighty Goliath. He fled for his life, but ultimately triumphed over the madness of King Saul. David knew his God experientially in the grit of battle and the daily humdrum.

What about you? Do you have a memory bank full of great experiences with God? If the answer is no, why not ask God for a deposit today? If you put your faith in him, he will not let you down.

RESPONSE

Lord, examine my heart and my mind. I want to grow in my knowledge of you and my confidence in you. Help me to have a pure heart and mind before you. I want to experience your presence in my life. Amen.

YOUR TURN

Have you experienced God's love and faithfulness recently? Do you let him examine you?

DAY 49: LOVE FOR THE HOUSE OF GOD

TODAY'S READING: PSALM 26:8–12

KEY VERSE: PSALM 26:8

LORD, I love the house where you live, the place where your glory dwells.

REFLECTION

In America, Canada, and much of the western world, people have been abandoning the house of God in droves. In the most recent census survey, the largest numerical growth has been among those who identify themselves as having no religion. This move away from religion is most pronounced among our young people. Jesus attracted people in his day. Why are his followers repelling people today? There are many factors that have led to this decline. Perhaps a hard look in the mirror is needed for us to see what we are doing wrong.

David had a completely different attitude toward the house of God. Hear the cry of his heart, "LORD, I love the house where you live, the place where your glory dwells."

No one had to drag David to the Lord's house. He was eager to meet with God there. Really, that's the secret. If God is in the house—if his glory is present—it will be hard to keep people away. The question we need to ask ourselves is, "Is God in the house? Is his glory dwelling here among us?"

If God is truly, tangibly present among you, look out! The transformational power of God will overwhelm individuals and ignite the congregation. I have seen that happen and there is no experience quite like it.

I live in expectation of his appearing among us. The living Christ visits his church. Are you anticipating his coming? Have you set the table for him? Have you prepared your heart and your mind? Have you put out the welcome mat?

Church today often has the wrong focus—one simply on program maintenance. Church in its most vibrant form is when God dwells among us—breathes upon us. That was the book of Acts church. That's the church I love. When we have found that place—when we experience the Lord of that place—we will join David in declaring, "My feet stand on level ground; in the great congregation I will praise the LORD" (v. 12).

RESPONSE

Come, Lord Jesus, dwell among us. This is my confession, "LORD, I love the house where you live, the place where your glory dwells" (v. 8). Lord, come and dwell in my local congregation. Manifest your presence there, so that many will see it and be changed by your Spirit. Amen.

YOUR TURN

Do you love the house of God? Why or why not? Is God showing up at your church? What are you doing to make the place ready for him?

DAY 50: ARE YOU AFRAID OF THE DARK?

TODAY'S READING: PSALM 27:1–3

KEY VERSE: PSALM 27:1

The LORD is my light and my salvation—whom shall I fear? The LORD is the stronghold of my life—of whom shall I be afraid?

REFLECTION

Are you afraid of the dark? That may seem like a rather empty-headed question. Most adults have overcome their fear of the dark a long time ago, back in the dark ages of childhood. But have you really overcome your fear of dark places?

I would like to suggest we have not overcome this most basic of fears. We have only learned to mask our fears and conveniently avoid those dark, unknown recesses. Our fear of the dark is, at its core, a fear of the unknown. Hidden out there in the dark, unknown regions is a whole battalion of hidden risks—the lurking boogeymen—who keep us close to home, who keep us on the well-beaten path, the well-marked path, a path of no risk and least resistance. How often do you dare to go where others have never gone? Are you still certain you are not afraid of the dark?

In this psalm, David, the fearless warrior, reveals the secret to his victorious life—a life spent overcoming insurmountable obstacles. With reckless confidence, this insignificant, no-rank shepherd boy took on the Goliaths of his time, and he rose to each and every challenge, time after time throughout his storied career.

So then, what was the secret to David's success? His success resides in his overwhelming confidence in the Lord. Surely, common sense would dictate that a wet-behind-the-ears shepherd boy is no match for an experienced warrior, such as the towering Goliath. But David exudes confidence. "The LORD is my light and my salvation—whom shall I fear? The LORD is the stronghold of my life—of whom shall I be afraid?" (v. 1).

David was not afraid of the dark, or the giant, or the Philistine army arrayed against him. He feared only the Lord. The Lord was his light in a dark place. The Lord was his salvation in every battle and his deliverance in every hostile situation. He bowed in reverential awe before him. He allied himself with the Lord, his Maker. That's an unbeatable combination.

RESPONSE

Lord Jesus, help me to truly walk in confident faith. I ally myself with you. You are my light and my salvation. Help me now to face my day and my future with confidence that comes from you, my Savior. Amen.

YOUR TURN

How often do you take a plunge into the unknown? Is God asking you to take a step of faith?

DAY 51: ARE YOU AT HOME WITH THE LORD?

TODAY'S READING: PSALM 27:4–6

KEY VERSE: PSALM 27:4

One thing I ask of the LORD, this only do I seek: that I may dwell in the house of the LORD all the days of my life, to gaze on the beauty of the LORD and seek him in his temple.

REFLECTION

No matter where we travel, or how pleasant the journey, within us all there is a longing to be home. The same longing for the safety and comfort of home can be found in this psalm of David. But for David, being at home meant being in the presence of God. The Lord God was David's refuge and comfort. To be near the Lord was to be safe, at rest, and fully at peace. Nearness to God was the paramount desire of David's heart.

Now hear David's heart cry, "One thing I ask of the LORD, this only do I seek: that I may dwell in the house of the LORD all the days of my life, to gaze on the beauty of the LORD and seek him in his temple."

David's statement here delineates a clear priority. For David, the house of the Lord was of first importance. I do not believe, however, that the physical structure or house was what attracted and captivated David. It was the Lord of the house who captured David's heart. He wanted to be with him. He longed to see the Lord and be at home in his house.

Like many preschool children, my youngest son Joshua had some difficulty pronouncing the *T H* sound. In his four-year-old vocabulary, the word "with" became "whiff" instead. He would make odd sounding statements such as this, "Daddy, I want to come whiff you," or, "I want to do that whiff you." Doing something "whiff" someone brings to mind the notion of being so close to them you can smell each other. That's close—really close. Bone of my bone and flesh of my flesh close—father and son close—intimate in a family kind of way.

Something deep and soul changing transpired as David tended that flock of sheep on those Judean hillsides. In his youth, David met God. The Lord was "whiff David," so close they could smell each other. In his youth, David tasted and saw that the Lord is good. Now, in his adult years, he yearned for that intimacy. He yearned for the house of the Lord. He was filled with a longing for home.

RESPONSE

Lord Jesus, I want to be "whiff" you. I want to live my life close to you now and close to you forever. Show me how to do that. Be near me, Lord Jesus. I ask you to stay close by me forever, and love me, I pray. Amen.

YOUR TURN

Are you at home with the Lord now? How at home will we feel with him in eternity if we aren't at home with him now?

DAY 52: DOES GOD HEAR ME WHEN I PRAY?

TODAY'S READING: PSALM 27:7–14

KEY VERSE: PSALM 27:7

Hear my voice when I call, LORD; be merciful to me and answer me.

REFLECTION

Is God listening? Do I have his full attention? Is he even there? Even people of great faith ask questions such as these. Listen to David's plea, "Hear my voice when I call, LORD."

David's psalms are replete with calls for God to listen and then quickly respond to his cries for help. These pleas for a listening ear happen with such frequency throughout the book of Psalms that one can be forgiven for wondering if God is deaf. In our minds, we know this is an absurd proposition. He who formed the ear can surely hear the faintest whispered prayer or unvoiced thought. But despite what our intellect knows, we still plead for his listening ear. Along with David, we cry out, "Hear my voice when I call, LORD; be merciful to me and answer me."

I suspect the problem in prayer is not that we are speaking to a deaf God, but rather we, the petitioners, are deaf to God's answers. The patriarchs and prophets of old heard the voice of God. They conversed with the Lord Almighty. Many of these conversations are recorded verbatim in the Old Testament. A fine example of this is found in Exodus 3 as Moses speaks with the Lord at the burning bush.

Have we lost the ability to hear God? Has a great collective deafness settled across humanity?

In a cold world filled with rejection, there is God—a God of mercy who the lonely soul can turn to. There is one who understands. There is one who listens to our anguished prayers. David discovered and knew that reality. We can join with David and say, "Though my mother and father forsake me, the LORD will receive me" (Psalm 27:10).

RESPONSE

Lord God, this is my confession, "I remain confident of this: I will see the goodness of the LORD in the land of the living" (Psalm 27:13). I will, "Wait for the LORD." I will, "Be strong and take heart and wait for the LORD" (v. 14). Amen.

YOUR TURN

Are there times when you doubt God is listening to your prayers? How do you know he is listening? Has the Lord spoken to your heart?

DAY 53: DO YOU WANT JUSTICE IN THIS LIFE?

TODAY'S READING: PSALM 28:1–5

KEY VERSE: PSALM 28:3

Do not drag me away with the wicked, with those who do evil, who speak cordially with their neighbors but harbor malice in their hearts.

REFLECTION

David begins Psalm 28 with a plea for God to hear him. As the psalm progresses, it becomes clear this is a plea not only for mercy, but also for justice. "Hear my cry for mercy as I call to you for help, as I lift up my hands toward your Most Holy Place. Do not drag me away with the wicked, with those who do evil, who speak cordially with their neighbors but harbor malice in their hearts" (vv. 2–3).

The cry for fairness is perhaps the most universal of all human desires. What is the most oft repeated phrase in a kindergarten class? If you guessed, "That's not fair!" you win the gold star. A desire for equality of opportunity and fairness is simply part of our human constitution—it's bred into us.

Governments are defeated and revolutions happen when leaders fail the test of fairness and equality under the law. All too often we do not see justice served in this life. The murderous Pol Pot was never brought to justice though three million Cambodians died under his regime. On a personal level, you too may have suffered a grievous injustice. When we become aware of such offenses and heinous crimes, David's call for justice rings true and clear. "Repay them for their deeds and for their evil work; repay them for what their hands have done and bring back on them what they deserve" (v. 4).

The oppressed and the oppressor will meet the God of justice in the afterlife. But the redeemed have this assurance, "'He will wipe every tear from their eyes. There will be no more death' or mourning or crying or pain, for the old order of things has passed away" (Revelation 21:4).

RESPONSE

Lord God, have mercy on me. "Do not drag me away with the wicked, with those who do evil." I put my trust in the redeeming sacrifice of your Son, Jesus. You are my help and salvation. Amen.

YOUR TURN

When you see injustice around you, do you take it to God in prayer? Are there other biblical ways to respond to injustice?

DAY 54: A COME FROM BEHIND OLYMPIC VICTORY

TODAY'S READING: PSALM 28:6–9

KEY VERSE: PSALM 28:7

The LORD is my strength and my shield; my heart trusts in him, and he helps me. My heart leaps for joy, and with my song I praise him.

REFLECTION

David ends Psalm 28 with a doxology of praise. Yes, it is good and fitting to praise the Lord. He hears our cry for mercy. To those who seek to know him, he is not a God of harsh judgment, or we would all perish. He is my shield and strength despite my frequent failings. David declares, "My heart trusts in him, and he helps me." I can join in David's declaration and personally testify to the truth of these words, "My heart trusts in him, and he helps me."

Our God does not stand afar off. He is near to those who call on him.

David was not one to be shy or reserved in his expression of praise. He exults, "My heart leaps for joy, and with my song I praise him." When David brought the Ark of the Covenant to Jerusalem, he gave full expression to his joy. "Wearing a linen ephod, David was dancing before the LORD with all his might, while he and all Israel were bringing up the ark of the LORD with shouts and the sound of trumpets" (2 Samuel 6:14–15).

Recently, I watched as Canada's women's Olympic hockey team scored a late-rally, come-from-behind, overtime victory over a shocked American team. There was no shortage of leaping, dancing, and rejoicing in the Canadian ranks. The outburst of praise and jubilation was completely fitting for them.

As born-again children of God, redeemed by the blood of the Lamb, we have a far greater reason—an eternal reason—for bursting forth in praise. Our Savior, the Lord Jesus Christ has scored a late-rally, come-from-behind, overtime victory over death, hell, and the grave. And he scored that victory for you and me. Together we are on an international team—Team Believer—believers in Jesus. What a victory he has won! What a celebration!

We join with David in declaring, "The LORD is the strength of his people, a fortress of salvation for his anointed one" (Psalm 28:8).

RESPONSE

Lord God, help me to grasp the full extent of the victory I have in you. Now, I ask you to hear my prayer, "Save your people and bless your inheritance; be their shepherd and carry them forever" (v. 9). Amen.

YOUR TURN

Why do we put limits on our expressions of praise to God, when our praise is exuberant and boundless at sporting events?

DAY 55: A PLACE OF PEACE DURING THE STORM

TODAY'S READING: PSALM 29

KEY VERSE: PSALM 29:9

The voice of the LORD twists the oaks and strips the forests bare. And in his temple all cry, "Glory!"

REFLECTION

In Psalm 29, we see and hear the Lord, the God of the storm. There is an evocative poetic style to this psalm that helps the reader to picture the fury of the approaching tempest. But we not only see the flashes of lightning and the power of the wind, we also hear the booming thunder as it shakes the desert. "The voice of the LORD twists the oaks and strips the forests bare. And in his temple all cry, 'Glory!'"

Seven times the psalmist repeats the phrase "the voice of the LORD." In this psalm, "the voice of the LORD" is a very active force. The voice of the Lord thunders, breaks, strikes, shakes, twists, and strips. The voice of the Lord is powerful. The voice of the Lord is majestic.

The voice of the Lord spoke the world into existence, set the planets in their orbits, and scattered the starry hosts across the heavens. A thunderstorm sweeping down from

Lebanon is as nothing to him.

But the Lord of the storm is also the Lord of peace. One day on the Sea of Galilee, Jesus our Lord brought peace to the storm.

> A furious squall came up, and the waves broke over the boat, so that it was nearly swamped. Jesus was in the stern, sleeping on a cushion. The disciples woke him and said to him, "Teacher, don't you care if we drown?"
>
> He got up, rebuked the wind and said to the waves, Quiet! Be still! Then the wind died down and it was completely calm." (Mark 4:37–39)

RESPONSE

God, you are the Lord of the storm and the Lord of peace. When storms arise in my life, help me to trust you completely. Lord Jesus, grant me peace in the midst of the storm. Amen.

YOUR TURN

Jesus says to us, "Why are you so afraid? Do you still have no faith?" (Mark 4:40). Do you hear him?

DAY 56: WHY SHOULD I PRAISE GOD?

TODAY'S READING: PSALM 30:1–5

KEY VERSE: PSALM 30:1

I will exalt you, LORD, for you lifted me out of the depths and did not let my enemies gloat over me.

REFLECTION

If you ever want an excuse to break out in praise, just read the opening lines of Psalm 30. There are plenty of excellent reasons to praise God, and David gives us several of them right here. "I will exalt you, LORD, for you lifted me out of the depths and did not let my enemies gloat over me."

The Lord has lifted me out of the depths of sin and the pit of discouragement on more than one occasion. Furthermore, the Lord provides more than just forgiveness. He also gives victory over the sin and the discouragement that entraps us. Through the death and resurrection of Jesus, he has defeated the minions of hell. Praise the Lord!

"LORD my God, I called to you for help, and you healed me" (v. 2). If you enjoy good health, praise the Lord. He is your healer. Whether through miraculous means or natural process, God is our healer, and we can thank him for the strength, energy, and rejuvenation he brings into our lives. Praise the Lord!

"You, LORD, brought me up from the realm of the dead; you spared me from going down to the pit" (v. 3).

In Ephesians, chapter 2, Paul tells us we were dead in trespasses and sins.

> But because of his great love for us, God, who is rich in mercy, made us alive with Christ even when we were dead in transgressions—it is by grace you have been saved. And God raised us up with Christ and seated us with him in the heavenly realms in Christ Jesus, in order that in the coming ages he might show the incomparable riches of his grace, expressed in his kindness to us in Christ Jesus. (Ephesians 2:4–7)

Praise the Lord!

We serve a God of mercy, redemption, and turnarounds. He turns our mourning into dancing (see Psalm 30:11). "For his anger lasts only a moment, but his favor lasts a lifetime; weeping may stay for the night, but rejoicing comes in the morning" (Psalm 30:5). Praise the Lord!

RESPONSE

Lord God, I thank you for your mercy and grace. I praise you for being my healer. You are good to me in more ways than I can count. Thank you. You are worthy of continual praise. Amen.

YOUR TURN

What can you praise God for today? How numerous are your blessings?

DAY 57: THE GOD OF SUDDEN TURNAROUNDS

TODAY'S READING: PSALM 30:6–12

KEY VERSES: PSALM 30:11–12

> You turned my wailing into dancing; you removed my sackcloth and clothed me with joy, that my heart may sing your praises and not be silent. Lord my God, I will praise you forever.

REFLECTION

Every psalm in the book of Psalms reveals to us an aspect or characteristic of God. Here in Psalm 30, we see the Lord God of mercy, redemption, and sudden turnarounds.

We all go through times of triumph as well as times of deep discouragement. My emotional life often swings between these two extremes. Some days my glass is half full and other days it's half empty. My faith level soars and plummets, often quite abruptly depending on circumstances. David also experienced these swings between optimism and pessimism. They are a trademark of his psalms. Perhaps that's why I love them. They reflect my own life experience.

In the opening lines of today's reading, David swings between a position of utter confidence and security to a position of shaken dismay. When trouble or disaster strikes, we may well ask, "Where is God in all this?" Like David we may call out, "'What is gained if I am silenced, if I go down to the pit? Will the dust praise you? Will it proclaim your faithfulness? Hear, LORD, and be merciful to me; LORD, be my help'" (vv. 9–10).

God is always on his throne. He is not caught by surprise when you lose your job, a relationship breaks down, a pandemic strikes, or you suffer a great loss. He remains secure, but more than that he is a God of great mercy and sudden turnarounds. He is the Lord God of resurrection. He turned the disciples mourning into dancing when he raised Jesus from the dead. Always, always, always remember he can do the same for you. In the course of this psalm, God turned David around. Jesus is the resurrection artist. And furthermore, remember this. "Jesus Christ is the same yesterday and today and forever" (Hebrews 13:8).

RESPONSE:

You turned my wailing into dancing; you removed my sackcloth and clothed me with joy, that my heart may sing your praises and not be silent. LORD my God, I will praise you forever" (Psalm 30:11–12). Amen.

YOUR TURN

Has God turned around a seemingly impossible situation for you? Take a moment to remind yourself of those God sent turnarounds.

DAY 58: THE IMPORTANCE OF A PLACE OF REFUGE

TODAY'S READING: PSALM 31:1–5

KEY VERSE: PSALM 31:2

Turn your ear to me, come quickly to my rescue; be my rock of refuge, a strong fortress to save me.

REFLECTION

We all need a place of refuge. Here as David begins Psalm 31, he pleads with God to hear him, and become a rock of refuge for him. "Turn your ear to me, come quickly to my rescue; be my rock of refuge, a strong fortress to save me."

David spent many of his early years fleeing from King Saul. At other times, the Philistines were a threat. There were many occasions in which David needed a fortress—a rock of refuge from his enemies. Often, he found himself calling out for the Lord to rescue him.

Are we any different? We may not have physical enemies who are seeking to kill us, but in the spiritual realm, the demonic forces of hell are constantly seeking opportunities to trip us up, so they can launch their vicious assault. Trouble and affliction come to every human life. We are not immune simply because we have put our faith in Christ. We, too, need a safe place—a rock of refuge.

But the rock to which we flee is not an inanimate object, fixed and unmoving. No, we come to the living rock which is Christ. He travels with us on this earthly pilgrimage. The apostle Paul reminds us that even the people of Israel wandering in the wilderness were not alone. "They all ate the same spiritual food and drank the same spiritual drink; for they drank from the spiritual rock that accompanied them, and that rock was Christ" (1 Corinthians 10:3–4).

The veins of that rock are open wide for us. Jesus bled and died so we could experience new life and complete forgiveness. As he hung dying, Jesus called out to his Father with the words of this psalm. "Into your hands I commit my spirit" (Psalm 31:5). Now, that living rock accompanies you daily. God is the fount of forgiveness and a sure refuge in a time of need. Have you put your trust in him for your salvation now and in eternity?

RESPONSE

Lord God, I thank you for Jesus. You alone are my rock and my eternal fortress. Guide my spirit into the right path today. Keep me safe from the traps of the enemy. I trust in you. Amen.

YOUR TURN

Is Jesus your living rock? Why is the analogy of Jesus as a rock a comfort to you?

DAY 59: YOU HAVE SET MY FEET IN A SPACIOUS PLACE

TODAY'S READING: PSALM 31:6–8

KEY VERSE: PSALM 31:8

You have not given me into the hands of the enemy but have set my feet in a spacious place.

REFLECTION

David clearly lacked a sense of political correctness. The opening line of this psalm portion makes me want to cringe. "I hate those who cling to worthless idols" (v. 6). What an inflammatory remark. Hate has no place in our expression of Christian faith. Didn't David know we are to hate the sin, but love the sinner? Perhaps we should send David off to a course in sensitivity training.

Somehow, biblical David got away with making such a statement, and here we have it recorded in the pages of Holy Scripture for all to read. Hate is a less than desirable emotion, but is it warranted in certain instances? My Christian love for murdering rapists grows mighty thin at times, and I speak from a distance. If my wife was killed by an idolatrous, murdering rapist, I am not sure how I would respond. Christ-centered forgiveness is the right response, but gut-wrenching hate might well spring to life when life circumstances become more than we can handle. My capacity for forgiveness in severe circumstances remains untested. I dare not boast in my theoretical ability to forgive.

The second part of David's opening remark is of crucial importance. "I hate those who cling to worthless idols; as for me, I trust in the LORD" (v. 6).

Only trust in the Lord can break the crippling bondage of sin and hate. Vengeance belongs to the Lord, not to the seething heart tortured and taunted by anger. Secular author Malcolm Gladwell explores the extraordinary power of forgiveness in his most recent book, *David and Goliath*. Gladwell's thoughts and research on the topic make for an insightful read. He concludes that forgiveness has the power to turn the world upside down. That's the power we find in the gospel. Rather than be caught in the trap of ruinous hate, through the power of Christ, we can step into the liberty of forgiveness.

By the gracious Holy Spirit, we have the ability to choose love over hate. David's confession can then become our own, "I will be glad and rejoice in your love, for you saw my affliction and knew the anguish of my soul" (v. 7).

When we choose love over hate, forgiveness over vengeance, trust in God over reliance on our own ability, we defeat Satan, the true enemy of our soul. Then the Lord sets us at liberty in a spacious place. With David, we can declare, "You have not given me into the hands of the enemy but have set my feet in a spacious place" (v. 8).

RESPONSE

Lord God, thank you for your forgiveness. Help me to practice it daily. Give me a forgiving spirit like your Son, Jesus, who forgave those who crucified him (Luke 23:34). Amen.

YOUR TURN

Is there someone you need to forgive? Do it today.

DAY 60: FROM THE BOTTOM OF THE DRY WELL

TODAY'S READING: PSALM 31:9–13

KEY VERSE: PSALM 31:9

Be merciful to me, LORD, for I am in distress; my eyes grow weak with sorrow, my soul and body with grief.

REFLECTION

How often do you find yourself crying out for mercy as David does at the start of this psalm portion? I confess, daily, I need God's mercy. "Be merciful to me, LORD, for I am in distress; my eyes grow weak with sorrow, my soul and body with grief."

The desperate cry for help is a recurring theme throughout the Psalms. While there is plenty of rejoicing and praise for the Lord throughout the book of Psalms, time after time we also read about David and the other writers of the Psalms calling out to God for mercy. Often these cries for help seem as though David has stumbled into a dry well and has no one to rescue him. Only God can help. Only God will listen.

Is that where you find yourself? In this psalm portion, we see David experiencing a deep sense of abandonment. He feels alone with no one to help. He laments, "I am forgotten as though I were dead" (v. 12a).

How often have you felt this same way? But David's sense

of abandonment plumbs even greater depths. Not only does David feel the sting of rejection, but he also feels totally worthless. In his despair, he cries, "I have become like broken pottery" (v. 12b). It appears he has lost all sense of meaning and purpose to his life. He is abandoned, useless, and worthless.

Is that where you find yourself? Then, do as David did. Pour out your complaint to God. Call out to him. He is listening. He cares and he answers. The Lord has not changed.

RESPONSE

Lord God, have mercy on me. Come to my aid. When I stumble and fall into the dry well of despair, please come to my rescue. Help me see Jesus peering down at me. Loving Jesus, extend your hand of help. Amen.

YOUR TURN

Reflect on how God has helped you in the past. How has he pulled you out of a pit?

DAY 61: MY TIMES ARE IN YOUR HANDS

TODAY'S READING: PSALM 31:14–18

KEY VERSE: PSALM 31:15

My times are in your hands; deliver me from the hands of my enemies, from those who pursue me.

REFLECTION

Yesterday, I made a trip to the hospital to visit a neighbor who is dying due to a brain tumor. Today, I just returned from visiting another neighbor who is dying due to heart failure. This neighbor had a heart transplant about ten years ago, and now that heart is being rejected. She has less than a year to live. Making matters more dire, she has a thirteen-year-old son and a ten-year-old daughter. David spoke the truth when he declared, "My times are in your hands." We have no idea, no certainty, about what tomorrow will bring. Will the new day bring life or death, joy or sorrow, pain or ecstasy, excitement or boredom? Our times are in God's hands. We devise our plans, but ultimately the Lord determines the outcome. "Many are the plans in a person's heart, but it is the LORD's purpose that prevails" (Proverbs 19:21).

As if to prove my point, when I searched online for the Proverbs passage quoted above, I discovered Canada's former finance minister, Jim Flaherty, had suddenly died of a heart attack. While to non-Canadian readers the name Jim Flaherty may mean nothing, to those who live in "the true north strong and free," Mr. Flaherty was a well-known and well-respected leader who piloted Canada through the Great Recession with consummate skill. He retired just one month before his sudden passing. Mr. Flaherty's times were in God's hands.

We can easily forget our times are in God's hands. "It is God who judges: He brings one down, he exalts another" (Psalm 75:7). He determines the length of our days. That's why the opening words of this psalm portion are so important. David asserts, "But I trust in you, LORD; I say, 'You are my God'" (Psalm 31:14).

In life and in death, God is Lord. Put your trust in him for today, for tomorrow, and for all eternity.

RESPONSE

Lord God, I do not know what the future holds for me, but like David, I put my trust in you. Guide me in your ways. My life is in your hands. Amen.

YOUR TURN

How long do you think you have on this earth? Are you ready for eternity?

DAY 62: HOW GENEROUS IS YOUR GOD?

TODAY'S READING: PSALM 31:19–20

KEY VERSE: PSALM 31:19

How abundant are the good things that you have stored up for those who fear you, that you bestow in the sight of all, on those who take refuge in you.

REFLECTION

Our view of God is of crucial importance. This view will greatly influence how we live our lives on planet Earth. Is God a divine ogre waiting to pounce on us for the slightest transgression? Is he aloof, hard of hearing, out of touch, and out of reach? Does he stand opposed to your wishes and dreams—the nagging heavenly parent who frowns at your ambitions?

That's not David's view of God. David saw a caring Lord of heaven and earth, who was only too eager to bless those who sought refuge in him. That's why David exclaims, "How abundant are the good things that you have stored up for those who fear you that you bestow in the sight of all, on those who take refuge in you."

Think about this for a moment: God has a storehouse of good things just waiting for you. He has prepared a whole series of blessings he will lavish on those who fear him. Furthermore, the Lord will bestow those blessings in the sight of all—on all who seek shelter in the shadow of his wings. Now that's a picture of an amazing God.

What might some of those good things be? First and foremost, the Lord has an abundance of mercy set aside just for you. During unparalleled disaster, as a witness to the destruction of Jerusalem, the prophet Jeremiah rightly discerned the heart of the Lord. "Because of the LORD's great love we are not consumed, for his compassions never fail. They are new every morning; great is your faithfulness" (Lamentations 3:22–23). For Jeremiah, God was good all the time, even in disaster.

God has an abundance of love, peace, and joy set aside just for you. Tap into it. Drink deep of that goodness. It's there for you. "For the kingdom of God is not a matter of eating and drinking, but of righteousness, peace and joy in the Holy Spirit, because anyone who serves Christ in this way is pleasing to God and receives human approval" (Romans 14:17–18).

We serve a generous God—a God of grace who extends unmerited favor to us. In your mind, stop limiting his blessings. They are abundant, they are stored up for you, and they will manifest in the lives of those who love and fear him.

RESPONSE

Lord God, thank you for all the good things you have stored up for me, both temporal and spiritual. I rejoice in you! You are a generous God lavishing mercy on me through your son, Jesus. Amen.

YOUR TURN

How do you see God? Do you have the right perspective of him? Is he opposed to your wishes and dreams?

DAY 63: ARE YOU LIVING IN A CITY UNDER SIEGE?

TODAY'S READING: PSALM 31:21–24

KEY VERSE: PSALM 31:21

Praise be to the LORD, for he showed me the wonders of his love when I was in a city under siege.

REFLECTION

David ends Psalm 31 with a testimony to God's great love and mercy. Hear his declaration, "Praise be to the LORD, for he showed me the wonders of his love when I was in a city under siege. In my alarm I said, 'I am cut off from your sight!' Yet you heard my cry for mercy when I called to you for help" (vv. 21–22).

Are you living in a city under siege? My quick and simple answer is no. My city is not surrounded by enemy troops who are lobbing artillery shells down on my neighborhood. While in the physical sense that may be true, in the spiritual realm, my city is caught up in active warfare. Demonic forces are firing their missiles into my city every day. The airwaves and social media feeds are filled with smut and pornography. In the public square, Christian faith is routinely mocked and under attack. Atheists trumpet their cause with bestselling books and spew venom on any who dare to embrace the faith. Meanwhile, pop culture plunges headlong into the deep end of gothic horror, vampire blood lust, and zombie self-identification. Then, we stand back in amazement when those same young people lash out in murderous and deranged madness as happened when five young people were stabbed to death in Calgary or in my hometown when an eighteen-year-old killed his mother.

When you shun God and bed down with the devil, many will end up hurt. My city is under siege. However, with the help and grace of God, I will not succumb to the enemy's attack. I will emerge triumphant. David did. And here is his advice for you and me: "Love the LORD, all his faithful people!" (v. 23a).

David's advice is counterintuitive. Take your eyes off the enemy. Don't be mesmerized by the devil's devices and machinations. Your salvation comes from the Lord. Set your heart and your affections on him. "The LORD preserves those who are true to him, but the proud he pays back in full. Be strong and take heart, all you who hope in the LORD" (vv. 23b–24).

RESPONSE

Lord God, have mercy on me. I love you, Lord. Preserve me through the unfailing love of your Son, Jesus. I will "be strong and take heart" because I set my hope on you. Amen.

YOUR TURN

Do you feel that your faith is under attack? How do you respond? What are some ways you counter the attacks? Do you cower or advance?

DAY 64: BREAKING THE DAM

TODAY'S READING: PSALM 32:1–5

KEY VERSE: PSALM 32:5

Then I acknowledged my sin to you and did not cover up my iniquity. I said, "I will confess my transgressions to the LORD." And you forgave the guilt of my sin.

REFLECTION

A right relationship with God is like a flowing stream. In such a relationship, there is a natural giving to God that includes prayer, worship, time spent in his word, and periods of quiet communion. In turn, God, by the Holy Spirit, pours his peace, love, and joy into our lives. Just as trees naturally line a riverbank, there is a verdant fruitfulness that comes to the believer as that refreshing current is allowed to flow.

Sin acts like a boulder hindering the flow of God's Spirit in our lives. As more and more unrepented sin piles up, a dam is formed. Suddenly prayer stops. Worship and thanksgiving that once cascaded so freely from our lips comes to a halt. The Word of God becomes boring, and we find other interests. Times of quiet communion with our Maker are replaced by a search for other things like constant entertainment.

This is the state of David's soul at the start of this psalm. The flow has stopped. Where is the overflowing cup experience of Psalm 23? At this point, David's cup—his soul—is sitting stagnant. In the natural realm, any liquid left unstirred becomes foul as time goes by. David's spiritual life was turning into a swamp because of unconfessed sin.

But there was a turning point for David. "Then I acknowledged my sin to you and did not cover up my iniquity. I said, 'I will confess my transgressions to the LORD" (v. 5).

Confession breaks the dam. David verbally brought his sin out in the open before God. He acknowledged what God knew all along. You see, David's sin and my sin are never hidden from God. Our sin is always in plain sight of the Lord. But praise God! He forgives the guilt of our sin when we break the spiritual dam through confession. Repentance restores the flow.

RESPONSE

Lord God, have mercy on me. "I acknowledge my sin to you and do not cover up my iniquity." I need your forgiveness. I put my trust in the redeeming sacrifice of your Son, Jesus. Amen.

YOUR TURN

Has unconfessed sin dammed up the flow of prayer and worship in your life? What can you do to restore a life-giving flow in your relationship with God?

DAY 65: A GAME OF HIDE 'N' SEEK WITH GOD

TODAY'S READING: PSALM 32:6–7

KEY VERSE: PSALM 32:6

Therefore let all the faithful pray to you, while you may be found; surely the rising of the mighty waters will not reach them.

REFLECTION

In the previous stanza of this psalm, David received the amazing dam-busting forgiveness of God. He has just experienced a wonderful release from a load of guilt. Now, in his next breath, he has some advice for us. "Therefore let all the faithful pray to you, while you may be found."

We are to pray to God while he may be found. This raises some interesting questions. Is God unavailable at times? If God cannot be found, is he hiding? Furthermore, if God is hiding, where does he hide?

At this point, I feel like jumping to my feet, like a lawyer pleading a case in the court of reason, and shouting out, "I object! All that David has told us about God so far would lead us to believe God is always close at hand. Didn't David testify to this earlier in Psalm 23? He said the following words about the Lord his shepherd: "Even though I walk through the darkest valley, I will fear no evil, for you are with me" (v. 4). However, now it seems David is telling us there are times when God cannot be found. Which is it, David? It can't be both.

Ah, but it is both. This is one of those great divine paradoxes. God, who is near, even in my heart, can also be distant—light years away—both in time and space. There exists a perceived distance between us that can vary according to the state of my heart—according to the state of my relationship with God.

The fact remains we cannot see God though we see evidence of his handiwork all around us. Our infinitely complex human bodies and finely tuned senses are proof of his existence, yet we cannot see him. He is a hidden God, and when we walk beside him, we walk by faith and not by sight.

Repeatedly in the Scriptures, we are commanded to seek after the Lord. I find this to be a rather curious expression. We cannot see God, and yet we are commanded to seek him, as though he might suddenly appear over the next hill, or around the next bend in the road. Suddenly, in unexpected ways, we may encounter God. In reality, the Psalms are all about encounters with God. Psalm 19 began that way. Suddenly, the starry hosts began talking to David about God, declaring his glory. We may pick up the Bible, and suddenly it speaks to our deepest need—the need of the moment. We know this is the voice of God with a word specifically for us today. Even the ungodly people of this world recognize that people encounter God. They use expressions like, "He found God," to describe someone's conversion to faith in Christ. The Lord invites us to play the most amazing game: hide 'n' seek with God.

RESPONSE

Lord God, I want to seek after you. Show yourself to me today in this grand adventure called life. I want to have an encounter with you. I want to know what it means to be found by you. Amen.

YOUR TURN

Describe a recent encounter you've had with God. Did you sense his nearness or distance?

DAY 66: THE LORD SPEAKS

TODAY'S READING: PSALM 32:8–11

KEY VERSE: PSALM 32:8

I will instruct you and teach you in the way you should go; I will counsel you with my loving eye on you.

REFLECTION

In Psalm 32, God speaks back. David begins this psalm, and we clearly can hear his voice addressing us as he tells how wonderful it is to be forgiven. Then, David goes on to speak of his own struggle with unconfessed sin. Finally, he tells us of the great relief he experienced as he is pardoned and restored to a place of close fellowship with the Lord. Then, abruptly in verse eight, we hear a different voice. God is speaking, and he responds to what David has said. Through this psalm, David models true prayer. This psalm is two-way communication.

We have heard David's words. Now, let's hear God's words. "I will instruct you and teach you in the way you should go; I will counsel you with my loving eye on you."

Clearly, this is not the voice of David. David is not going to counsel and watch over us. This is the work of the Lord. The Lord will teach and guide us. It is his role to shepherd the flock of his pasture with his loving eye.

These words, from verse eight to the end of this psalm, are coming from the Lord. David has heard God speak, and now he is passing on this message from the Lord directly to us. In this respect, David is fulfilling the role of a prophet. He is acting as God's spokesperson. In fact, in Acts 2:30, Peter asserts that David was a prophet. What is a prophet? In the simplest terms, it is someone who hears God, and then passes on God's message to others.

Do you hear God? This is no idle, rhetorical question. Hearing the voice of God is essential to our Christian faith. I would go so far as to say you cannot experience salvation unless you first hear God. Jesus said, "My sheep listen to my voice; I know them, and they follow me. I give them eternal life, and they shall never perish" (John 10:27–28).

In short, we must be able to hear Jesus in order to follow him, and it is in following him that we receive eternal life. Hearing God's voice is of paramount importance.

RESPONSE

Lord God, give me ears to hear what you have to say to me. Please instruct me and teach me in the way I should go. Then give me grace to obey. I put my trust in you, O Lord. Amen.

YOUR TURN

Do you hear God's voice? How does he speak to you? Have you heard the Lord's voice recently? How do you distinguish God's voice from all the other voices you hear?

DAY 67: SING JOYFULLY TO THE LORD

TODAY'S READING: PSALM 33:1–5

KEY VERSE: PSALM 33:1

Sing joyfully to the LORD, you righteous; it is fitting for the upright to praise him.

REFLECTION

Waking up with a song of praise to the Lord on your lips is a great way to start your day. How do I know that's true? I listen to birds. Their joyous songs are new every morning. If they have cause to sing praise to the Lord, surely, I do as well.

Jesus said, "Are not two sparrows sold for a penny? Yet not one of them will fall to the ground outside your Father's care. And even the very hairs of your head are all numbered. So don't be afraid; you are worth more than many sparrows" (Matthew 10:29–31).

If a sparrow has grounds for praising the Lord each and every day, surely, we have more. His constant care sustains us moment by moment. If the Father keeps count of my hairs, he must be concerned about even the tiny details of my life. His loving mercy is new every morning, therefore, "it is fitting for the upright to praise him."

In Psalm 33:2 we are instructed to, "Praise the LORD with the harp; make music to him on the ten-stringed lyre."

Forgive me, Lord. I'm an instrumental disaster. Playing skillfully is nigh unto impossible. But with my voice, I will praise you. I can't compete with robins and cardinals, but I will sing my praise. "For the word of the LORD is right and true; he is faithful in all he does" (v. 4).

The steadfast love of the Lord is unchanging. My praise for him should be just as steadfast—unaffected by my current circumstances. I have heard the birds break into song at sunrise even on a gray, rainy morning. At the very least, my praise for God should be as constant. Paul and Silas sang praises to God after being severely flogged and imprisoned in Philippi (see Acts 16). Their worship was unaffected by their circumstances. They were obedient to the Lord's command, "Sing joyfully to the LORD, you righteous; it is fitting for the upright to praise him."

RESPONSE

Thank you, Lord God, for each day you set before me. Give me a heart of praise for you. You sustain me. Today give me a new song to praise you, O Lord. It's always good, right, and fitting to sing my praise to you. Amen.

YOUR TURN

When do you love to praise God? Does it lift your spirit when you do? Are there times when the Lord has given you a new song to sing?

DAY 68: THE CREATIVE POWER OF WORDS

TODAY'S READING: PSALM 33:6–9

KEY VERSE: PSALM 33:6

By the word of the LORD the heavens were made, their starry host by the breath of his mouth."

REFLECTION

Have you ever considered the creative power of words? Words change the world. They bring order out of chaos. Words shine the light of day into the darkness of this world. From the very beginning, words have been imbued with divine power. The psalmist reminds us, "By the word of the LORD the heavens were made, their starry host by the breath of his mouth."

But it's not only God's words that have this vast power. Our words, human words, whether spoken, written, or thought have enormous power too. Adam's first job assignment was to speak words—to name the animals. "Now the LORD God had formed out of the ground all the wild animals and all the birds in the sky. He brought them to the man to see what he would name them; and whatever the man called each living creature, that was its name. So the man gave names to all the livestock, the birds in the sky and all the wild animals" (Genesis 2:19–20).

Strangely, God didn't do what every parent does. He didn't tell Adam what the animals were called. Adam told God their names. By so doing, God vested mankind with the power of language. Life is what we call it. Our words describe the world and give meaning to it.

Through our words, we bring order and make sense of the world around us. As a writer, I am continually processing and attempting to make sense of this chaotic thing called life. I do it with words. From the beginning of time, by divine command, that's what we are called to do. We are to speak order into chaos—speak accuracy and clarity into this world's muddled reality.

With our words, we shine the light of truth onto a situation. With words, we write laws, administer justice, and design government. With words, we woo and romance and vow our love to one another. Our words create imaginary realms into which we can travel—words that transport. With our words, we have the power to elevate the human spirit, or crush someone to the point of suicide.

Finally, there is something innately prophetic about our words. What we think, speak, and write is potent. Our words have within them the latent ability to become reality. Therefore, we need to guard our lips (see James 3:1–12). The psalmist reminds us not only of the power of the Word of the Lord, but also our own words. "For he spoke, and it came to be; he commanded, and it stood firm" (Psalm 33:9).

RESPONSE

Lord God, help me give careful consideration to my words. Today, may my words, whether written or spoken, be a creative force for good in Jesus's name. Amen.

YOUR TURN

How has God used your words for good lately? Describe how your words can bring order out of chaos.

DAY 69: THE PLANS OF NATIONS

TODAY'S READING: PSALM 33:10–15

KEY VERSES: PSALM 33:10–11

The LORD foils the plans of the nations; he thwarts the purposes of the peoples. But the plans of the LORD stand firm forever, the purposes of his heart through all generations.

REFLECTION

I confess I am a bit of a history buff. I am currently reading *The War that Ended Peace* by Margaret MacMillan. The subtitle is *The Road to 1914*. As you might guess, it highlights the causes of World War I. Throughout, the author meticulously points out that war was not inevitable. A change in course by any of the key players in the years leading up to 1914 could have prevented this monumental catastrophe. Each nation had plans and objectives they considered in their best interest. Quite naturally, the pursuit of those plans led to conflict with neighboring nations with opposing objectives.

What does the psalmist say about national objectives? "The LORD foils the plans of the nations; he thwarts the purposes of the peoples. But the plans of the LORD stand firm forever, the purposes of his heart through all generations" (Psalm 34:10–11).

Nations pursue their own perceived national interest. Despite the rhetoric we sometimes hear, they do not pursue the plans and purposes of the Lord. For political leaders, national self-interest trumps the purposes of God. In fact, the purposes of God are seldom considered. "But the plans of the LORD stand firm forever, the purposes of his heart through all generations."

Was it God's plan and purpose for millions of Christian believers to be slaughtered in World War I? Many atheists claim this is what we believe. Yet, nothing could be further from the truth. We are responsible for our own actions. God does not cause war. Humans cause war, and they carry it out. Why should we suddenly blame God for what we have engineered through our own dogged stupidity? Blaming God for our own arrogant idiocy is the pinnacle of irresponsibility, yet we do it all the time, both on a national and a personal level. Most often, we are the author of our own disaster. We stubbornly fail to pull back and change course before it's too late.

"Blessed is the nation whose God is the LORD, the people he chose for his inheritance" (v. 12).

RESPONSE

Lord God, thank you for choosing me to be to be one of your people. Help me to live a life that is pleasing to you, my Father. You watch over me. You, O Lord, are my inheritance, and first and foremost I am a citizen of your eternal kingdom. Amen.

YOUR TURN

How does personal conflict escalate? Do you sometimes blame God rather than take personal responsibility?

DAY 70: IT'S ALL ABOUT HOPE

TODAY'S READING: PSALM 33:16–22

KEY VERSE: PSALM 33:16

No king is saved by the size of his army; no warrior escapes by his great strength.

REFLECTION

This final portion of Psalm 33 is all about hope. From the first breath we take, until our last gasp, life is all about hope. Life has no meaning or purpose if we lose hope.

The essential question we must ask is where do you place your hope? All too often we place our hope in the things of this world, our resources, our ingenuity, and the strength of our flesh. But the psalmist reminds us, "No king is saved by the size of his army; no warrior escapes by his great strength. A horse is a vain hope for deliverance; despite all its great strength it cannot save" (vv. 15–16).

Time and again throughout history, the little guy has won. David defeated Goliath. The Viet Cong ousted the US Army. The Afghan rebels outlasted the armies of the USSR. Victory does not always go to the mighty. So, the lament goes up, "How the mighty have fallen! The weapons of war have perished!" (2 Samuel 1:27).

Where is your hope? Where have you put your trust? The psalmist reminds us to put our hope in the Lord. Leaders come and go. Nations rise and fall. Human abilities wane. "The grass withers and the flowers fall, but the word of our God endures forever" (Isaiah 40:8).

Our hope and our trust must be in God and in his unfailing Word.

When calamity strikes, those who maintain hope survive. Those who give up hope perish. In stories of extreme survival, over and over again this truth is borne out. Hope sustains the human heart when food and water run out. When we put our trust in the Lord, we tap into a limitless supply of hope. Therefore: "We wait in hope for the Lord; he is our help and our shield. In him our hearts rejoice, for we trust in his holy name" (Psalm 33:20–21).

RESPONSE

This is our prayer. "May your unfailing love be with us, Lord, even as we put our hope in you" (v. 22). In the name of Jesus, our source of hope, who defeated death, we pray. Amen.

YOUR TURN

What are some sources of false hope? Why have you put your hope in God?

DAY 71: PRAISE FOR ANSWERED PRAYER

TODAY'S READING: PSALM 34:1–7

KEY VERSE: PSALM 34:6

This poor man called, and the LORD heard him;
he saved him out of all his troubles.

REFLECTION

David was a man of many talents. He was a gifted
musician and a poet—the author of many of the psalms.
He was a battle-hardened warrior and a leader of men.
After many years of struggle, he became the king of all
Israel, and in that role, he governed an unruly people with
wisdom, justice, and demonstrable success. David was also
a prophet. Many of his psalms are infused with prophetic
significance as they point to the coming Messiah—Jesus
Christ.

In addition to this long list of David's skills and
accomplishments, we should also add actor. In an early
episode in David's flight from King Saul, he escaped to the
Philistine city of Gath. But he was recognized by some of
the people who said, "'Isn't this David, the king of the land?
Isn't he the one they sing about in their dances: "Saul has
slain his thousands, and David his tens of thousands"?'" (1
Samuel 21:11).

To escape certain death, David pretended to be stark
raving mad. He must have been a convincing actor because
the king of Gath released him saying, "Look at the man! He
is insane! Why bring him to me? Am I so short of madmen

that you have to bring this fellow here to carry on like this in front of me? Must this man come into my house?" (1 Samuel 21:14–15).

In response to his release from King Achish, David composed Psalm 34—one of the most joyous of all the psalms. Nothing inspires praise like answered prayer when your life is on the line. David did not take the credit for his skill as an actor. Neither did he take credit for conceiving the idea for this clever deception. He gave all the glory to God and he invites us to join in his celebration of praise. "Glorify the LORD with me; let us exalt his name together. I sought the LORD, and he answered me; he delivered me from all my fears" (Psalm 34:3–4)

Along with David, we have good reason to rejoice—we have a God who saves us. "This poor man called, and the LORD heard him; he saved him out of all his troubles" (v. 6).

RESPONSE

"Those who look to him are radiant" (v. 5a). Lord, we look to you. Today, let me shine for you. Amen.

YOUR TURN

What talents can you thank God for? How has he answered your prayers?

DAY 72: WHAT DOES GOD TASTE LIKE?

TODAY'S READING: PSALM 34:8–14

KEY VERSE: PSALM 34:8

Taste and see that the LORD is good; blessed is the one who takes refuge in him.

REFLECTION

David begins this portion of Psalm 34 by urging us to "Taste and see that the LORD is good." What a strange command!

One can logically argue that of the five senses taste is the most intimate. I can see, hear, and even smell someone at a distance. Touch, of course, requires direct contact, but to taste someone or something, I must take it or them into my mouth. That's intimate.

How do I, "Taste and see that the LORD is good?" If I can't see, hear, smell, or touch the Lord, how can I possibly taste him? David goes on to state, "Blessed is the one who takes refuge in him" (v. 8b). Notice David did not say we are blessed if we take refuge *with* the Lord. We are to take refuge *in* him. That requires a higher level of intimacy—a marital kind of intimacy.

Do I taste and see that the Lord is good? Do I take refuge in him? Do I actively seek God? John Ortberg in his book *Know Doubt* tells us that C.S. Lewis said, "That speaking of man's search for God always sounded to him like speaking of the mouse's search for the cat." The mouse hides from the cat because he fears the cat may require his life. We avoid God for the same reason. If you find God, he may ask for your life. Are you willing to give it up to him?

Jesus was willing to give his life for you. He willingly suffered, bled, and died on a cross so that you might have eternal life. The big cat—the Lion of the Tribe of Judah—lay down his life for the mouse, even a mangy mouse like me. That's real love. Now, Jesus invites us to come and dine. Jesus said, "Whoever eats my flesh and drinks my blood has eternal life, and I will raise them up at the last day. For my flesh is real food and my blood is real drink. Whoever eats my flesh and drinks my blood remains in me, and I in them" (John 6:54–56).

RESPONSE

Heavenly Father, thank you for sending Jesus. Thank you, Jesus, for laying down your life for me. Through the sacrifice of your body and blood I can truly "taste and see that the Lord is good." Amen.

YOUR TURN

Do you seek God or avoid him? Why?

DAY 73: WHAT DOES GOD LOOK LIKE?

TODAY'S READING: PSALM 34:15–18

KEY VERSE: PSALM 34:15–16

The eyes of the LORD are on the righteous, and his ears are attentive to their cry; but the face of the LORD is against those who do evil, to blot out their name from the earth.

REFLECTION

In yesterday's discussion of Psalm 34, I asked the question, "What does God taste like?" Remember, David invites us in Psalm 34:8 to "Taste and see that the LORD is good."

As this psalm continues, David again invites us to take a closer look at God. He reminds us that, "The eyes of the LORD are on the righteous, and his ears are attentive to their cry; but the face of the LORD is against those who do evil to blot out their name from the earth."

In this passage, David depicts the Lord as having eyes, ears, and a face. I always have trouble picturing God. This inability does not stem from a lack of imagination. It comes from the knowledge that God is a spirit. How do you picture something that has no physical substance or form?

But picturing God comes with further difficulties. We are specifically forbidden to create an image or likeness of God. The God of the Hebrews sat on the Mercy Seat on the Ark of the Covenant between two cherubim, but there was no image or statue there. To create an image or statue would be blasphemous. For that reason, I find Michelangelo's painting on the ceiling of the Sistine Chapel offensive. I am not offended by the depiction of a naked Adam. I'm offended by the portrayal of an old gray-haired man as God. How dare he create an image of God? I am similarly troubled by any artistic rendering of God the Father. God is so far beyond human that to render him as having a human form demeans his majesty.

But that's what makes the incarnation so spectacular. This God of no fixed form took on material reality. In the person of Jesus, he became a man with eyes, ears, and a human face. The God who sees all and hears all limited himself to a human body. The Creator took on the form and limitations of a creature—limitations that encompass betrayal, pain, and death. In the body of Jesus, the Creator God, who sees and hears, experienced our reality—our humanity.

The psalmist, David declares, "The righteous cry out, and the LORD hears them; he delivers them from all their troubles. The LORD is close to the brokenhearted and saves those who are crushed in spirit" (vv. 17–18).

The Lord is close to the brokenhearted, because in the form of Christ, his heart was broken. He experienced the pain that touches you and more. His eyes are on you. He is listening when you cry out.

RESPONSE

Hear my prayer, Lord. I seek your face. Be my healer, my redeemer, and deliverer. In the name of Jesus, who defeated death, I pray. Amen.

YOUR TURN

Do you have a picture of God? How does God look to you?

DAY 74: DO YOU WANT A TROUBLE-FREE LIFE?

TODAY'S READING: PSALM 34:19–22

KEY VERSE: PSALM 34:19

The righteous person may have many troubles, but the LORD delivers him from them all.

REFLECTION

This final portion of Psalm 34 reflects David's faith in a God who saves. He began this psalm with praise because he had experienced the saving power of God. Now, David states that the Lord delivers, protects, and rescues. For these words to be meaningful, the Lord must deliver, protect, and rescue from various forms of trouble and adversity. There is no rescue if there is no danger. There is no deliverance if there is no oppression.

If you choose to follow the Lord, you are not guaranteed a trouble-free life. Jesus told his disciples, "In this world you will have trouble. But take heart! I have overcome the world" (John 16:33).

Many of us believe if we do our best to lead a good life, following the commandments as found in the Bible, God will exempt us from hardship and trouble. But Jesus, the sinless Son of God, did not have a trouble-free life. Why should we expect our lives to be trouble free? God has not promised me a trouble-free life. He has promised to be with me when trouble and adversity comes.

About six years ago, a close friend of mine suffered a debilitating stroke. He lost his position as a teacher, his finances took a hit, and he struggled mightily to regain his mobility. In an instant, every movement became much more difficult for him—every step a monumental effort. Last week, he made a startling confession. He said, "If I had it to do over, I wouldn't go back. I wouldn't return to my pre-stroke days. God has drawn me so much closer to himself through this. I wouldn't wish this on any man, but God has changed me and used me in new ways that wouldn't have been possible unless this happened."

All of us desperately try to avoid the furnace of affliction. It's too hard, too unpleasant, and too full of things we cannot bear. But God meets us there. He bears us up on eagle's wings. When our resources and abilities run out, he takes over. He becomes our help and our deliverer in ways we cannot fathom. God is present in times of trouble.

His promises are tried, tested, and true. "The LORD will rescue his servants; no one who takes refuge in him will be condemned" (Psalm 34:22).

RESPONSE

Heavenly Father, I can't always see what is genuinely in my best interest, especially when that involves adversity. Be my sure help and protection in troubled times. "May your unfailing love be with us, LORD, even as we put our hope in you" (v. 22). In Jesus's name, we pray. Amen.

YOUR TURN

Has God met with you in a time of trouble? Do you know him as your strength and rescuer in times of hardship and difficulty? Reflect on times God helped you.

DAY 75: IS GOD ON YOUR SIDE?

TODAY'S READING: PSALM 35:1–6

KEY VERSE: PSALM 35:1

Contend, LORD, with those who contend with me;
fight against those who fight against me.

REFLECTION

David was a man acquainted with warfare. Throughout his life, Israel was in a prolonged struggle with its neighbors, even as it is today. From time to time, this struggle would flare into open combat. Quite naturally in those times, David would turn to the Lord in prayer. Psalm 35 is David's call for help against his enemies—enemies that may be external or internal.

Who doesn't want God on their side? The answer is obvious: we all want God's help when we find ourselves in trouble. Therefore, David cries out, "Contend, LORD, with those who contend with me; fight against those who fight against me."

There are some questions, however, we should ask ourselves before we enlist the Lord's help. Am I being truthful? Is my cause just? Do I know all the facts in this matter? Am I seeing this issue solely from a narrow, personal perspective? Finally, we should ask ourselves if our heart is right. One can be totally right about a matter, but have a heart that is full of hate, bitterness, jealousy, and anger.

God always stands on the side of truth and justice. He knows the full extent of a matter. He sees all sides, not just our perspective. We can't fool him or hide from his searching eyes. "The LORD examines the righteous, but the wicked, those who love violence, he hates with a passion" (Psalm 11:5). Therefore, we need to come before him humbly with hearts opened wide.

David asks this of the Lord, "*Say to me,* 'I am your salvation'" (Psalm 35:3 emphasis mine).

The Lord will be our salvation. He is on our side if our hearts are open and humble before him. David's confession in Psalm 51 confirms this truth. "My sacrifice, O God, is a broken spirit; a broken and contrite heart you, God, will not despise" (Psalm 51:17). In other words, God is on our side when we move to his side in honest, humble contrition.

RESPONSE

Lord God, give me a humble heart that sees beyond my narrow interests. Help me to stand for righteousness, justice, and truth. First, I want to align my heart and my spirit with you. In the name of Jesus, I pray. Amen.

YOUR TURN

Describe a time the Lord fought on your side. Did you need to get your heart right first?

DAY 76: HELP IN THE BATTLES WE ALL FACE

TODAY'S READING: PSALM 35:7–10

KEY VERSE: PSALM 35:9

Then my soul will rejoice in the LORD and delight in his salvation.

REFLECTION

The apostle Paul reminds us, as believers in the Lord Jesus Christ, we are engaged in spiritual warfare. "Put on the full armor of God, so that you can take your stand against the devil's schemes. For our struggle is not against flesh and blood, but against the rulers, against the authorities, against the powers of this dark world and against the spiritual forces of evil in the heavenly realms. Therefore put on the full armor of God, so that when the day of evil comes, you may be able to stand your ground, and after you have done everything, to stand" (Ephesians 6:11–13).

The conflicts David experienced in the Old Testament, reflected in the words of this portion of Psalm 35, are mirrored in the spiritual warfare experienced by New Testament believers. Make no mistake—the devil and his cohorts have dug a pit to trap you. They spread their nets to ensnare you in sin and degradation. But as was true for David, the Lord has also provided a way of escape for you and me. Once again, Paul reminds us of this: "No temptation has overtaken you except what is common to mankind. And God is faithful; he will not let you be tempted beyond what you can bear. But when you are tempted, he will also provide a way out so that you can endure it" (1 Corinthians 10:13).

The Lord has equipped us with the armor of God, and he has provided a way of escape. So, like David, we can rejoice in the victory the Lord will bring.

"Then my soul will rejoice in the LORD and delight in his salvation. My whole being will exclaim, 'Who is like you, LORD? You rescue the poor from those too strong for them, the poor and needy from those who rob them'" (Psalm 35:9–10).

Satan is a thief and a robber. He robs us of victory, peace, and joy. But like David and Paul, we can overcome. Victory is possible because the victory has already been won for us at the cross, and it was confirmed on resurrection morning at the empty tomb. "Thanks be to God, who delivers me through Jesus Christ our Lord!" (Romans 7:25).

RESPONSE

Heavenly Father, I thank you for the armor you have provided so I can stand against the wiles of the devil. I praise you for the power of your holy word. I have victory through your blood, Lord Jesus. Amen.

YOUR TURN

In your battle against sin are you using "the sword of the Spirit, which is the word of God" (Ephesians 6:17)? What are you doing to keep your sword sharp?

DAY 77: DO YOU STAND ACCUSED?

TODAY'S READING: PSALM 35:11–16

KEY VERSE: PSALM 35:12

They repay me evil for good and leave me like one bereaved.

REFLECTION

There is a prophetic, messianic element to today's Psalm 35 reading. Historically, on several occasions, close friends viciously turned on David. During Absalom's rebellion, David was betrayed not only by his son, but also by his confidants, who repaid his kindness with evil. He was openly mocked and tormented by Shimei, son of Gera, as he fled Jerusalem (see 2 Samuel 16:5–14). Though this is part of David's experience, this psalm portion also has its prophetic fulfillment in the slanderous betrayal of Christ.

Matthew records, "The chief priests and the whole Sanhedrin were looking for false evidence against Jesus so that they could put him to death. But they did not find any, though many false witnesses came forward" (Matthew 26:59–60).

After being betrayed by Judas, his own disciple, Jesus was mocked, stripped, and beaten by Roman soldiers (Matthew 27:27–31). While nailed to a cross, the crowd hurled abuse at him. "In the same way the chief priests, the teachers of the law and the elders mocked him. 'He saved others,' they said, 'but he can't save himself! He's the king of Israel! Let him come down now from the cross, and we will believe in him. He trusts in God. Let God rescue him now if he wants him, for he said, "I am the Son of God."' In the same way the rebels who were crucified with him also heaped insults on him" (Matthew 27:41–44).

The shrieking crowds of hell heaped abuse onto our Savior. Those same demonic crowds are ready to hurl their accusations at us when we stumble. Satan, our accuser, delights in tormenting us by bringing up the sins of our past. He mocks our efforts at change, insisting that it can't be done. But he is wrong—dead wrong. "I can do all this through him who gives me strength" (Philippians 4:13).

The accuser only has power over us if we listen to his lies. Our victory is in the risen Christ!

RESPONSE

Jesus, you are my victory when the enemy accuses me. I put my trust in your redeeming blood. Help me to stand firm against the taunts of the enemy. Amen.

YOUR TURN

Who do you turn to when you feel you have been betrayed or wrongly accused?

DAY 78: LEARNING IN THE "SCHOOL OF HARD KNOCKS"

Today's Reading: Psalm 35:17–21

Key Verse: Psalm 35:17

How long, Lord, will you look on? Rescue me from their ravages, my precious life from these lions.

REFLECTION

This portion of Psalm 35 begins with David's cry for help, "How long, Lord, will you look on? Rescue me from their ravages, my precious life from these lions."

When I am in distress, help can never arrive too soon. I want an instant answer from God. Better yet, he should have preempted this disappointment—this disaster. But often God doesn't instantly ride to our rescue. If poor choices are the cause of our distress, he may let us experience the consequences of our folly. When you are enrolled in the "School of Hard Knocks," the test comes first, and then you learn the lesson. Often patient endurance brings about an invaluable change in character through the work of the Holy Spirit. James, the brother of our Lord, reminds us of this truth:

"Consider it pure joy, my brothers and sisters, whenever you face trials of many kinds, because you know that the testing of your faith produces perseverance. Let perseverance finish its work so that you may be mature and complete, not lacking anything" (James 1:2–4).

However, all our troubles do not come as a result of bad decisions on our part. "Yet man is born to trouble as surely as sparks fly upward" (Job 5:7). Job reminds us that even the good and the just will at times face suffering. Anyone who tells you differently is not being faithful to the full counsel of Scripture. Satan severely tested Job, but he remained firm in his faith.

When hardships come will you stand firm? When the haughty accuse, can you bear it? David and Jesus felt the sting of false accusation. "They sneer at me and say, 'Aha! Aha! With our own eyes we have seen it'" (Psalm 35:21).

Thanks be to God. We can bring our trials and burdens to the Lord in prayer. He hears and in his perfect time, he responds.

RESPONSE

Lord, you know the troubles and trials I face daily. You are my help and my strength. "I will give you thanks in the great assembly; among the throngs I will praise you" (v. 18). Amen.

YOUR TURN

Do you learn from God's word, from the "School of Hard Knocks," or from both?

DAY 79: ARE YOU A PEACEMAKER?

TODAY'S READING: PSALM 35:22–25

KEY VERSES: PSALM 35:22–23

LORD, you have seen this; do not be silent. Do not be far from me, Lord. Awake, and rise to my defense! Contend for me, my God and LORD.

REFLECTION

There's an old saying, "The more things change, the more they stay the same." That certainly is true of the conflict in the Holy Land. About three thousand years ago, in David's time, the Kingdom of Israel was in a struggle for survival. Chief among its enemies were the Philistines along the Gaza coast. As I wrote this devotion, Israel's chief enemy Hamas is firing rockets into Israel from the Gaza coast.

David's words from Psalm 35 have a present-day resonance. "Lord, you have seen this; do not be silent. Do not be far from me, Lord. Awake, and rise to my defense! Contend for me, my God and Lord." Many in present day Israel are praying this prayer with the fervor of those who are being attacked.

But the residents of Gaza could pray this prayer with equal fervor. Their homes and businesses are also under bombardment. Where is God in all this suffering? Whose side is he on? Many in the Christian community affirm with great confidence that God is on the side of Israel. Does that make God complicit in the deaths of innocent children in Gaza?

Jesus gave this counsel to his disciples, "You have heard that it was said, 'Eye for eye, and tooth for tooth.' But I tell you, do not resist an evil person. If anyone slaps you on the right cheek, turn to them the other cheek also" (Matthew 5:38–39). Present day Israel (and America, for that matter) has a well-established policy of hard-hitting retaliation when attacked. What are the long-term consequences of this policy? Is the conflict resolved or is it inflamed?

Christ's admonition to turn the other cheek goes unheeded. Most feel that turning the other cheek implies weakness. In reality, it requires far more strength. However, in the end, it yields the peaceable fruit of righteousness—not a righteousness that insists on its own way—but a righteousness that sees both sides of an issue and works hard for peace and reconciliation.

Jesus asks us to do the far harder thing. Retaliation is easy and is often the natural response. Forgiving when we are wronged requires far more effort. Whose side is God on? He is on the side of peace. That's something worth fighting for.

RESPONSE

"Blessed are the peacemakers, for they will be called children of God" (Matthew 5:9). Lord God, help me to be a local peacemaker in my world today—someone who builds bridges between people and communities. Amen.

YOUR TURN

Forgiveness and turning the other cheek works on a personal level. How can we make it work on a community, interracial, and international level as well?

DAY 80: WE ADVANCE OURSELVES BY ADVANCING OTHERS

TODAY'S READING: PSALM 35:26–28

KEY VERSE: PSALM 35:26

May all who gloat over my distress be put to shame and confusion; may all who exalt themselves over me be clothed with shame and disgrace.

REFLECTION

Psalm 35 draws to a close with this warning against *schadenfreude*: "May all who gloat over my distress be put to shame and confusion; may all who exalt themselves over me be clothed with shame and disgrace."

What is schadenfreude? Dictionary.com defines "schadenfreude" as "satisfaction or pleasure felt at someone else's misfortune." It is a compound German word: *schaden* or harm plus *freude* or joy. In other words, schadenfreude is the joy you may feel when hearing about another person's calamity.

Schadenfreude can be viewed as the ladder climber's delight in seeing others fall behind or off the ladder entirely. Far too often, schadenfreude manifests in the false assumption that we can advance ourselves by putting others down. The truth is we advance ourselves by advancing others. Advancing by putdowns, insults, jibes, or criticism has no firm foundation because doing so hurts others and creates hostility. In addition, using these techniques usually ends badly because pride precedes a fall, just as darkness follows sunset.

The apostle Paul gives us this advice: "Bless those who persecute you; bless and do not curse. Rejoice with those who rejoice; mourn with those who mourn. Live in harmony with one another. Do not be proud, but be willing to associate with people of low position. Do not be conceited" (Romans 12:14–16).

Take joy in the success of others rather than resenting their achievements. Let their successes ignite within you a desire for self-improvement. With God's help, change what you can within yourself before looking to change others. We all have a place in our heart that needs some renovation.

Then with David, we can rejoice when others succeed. "May those who delight in my vindication shout for joy and gladness; may they always say, 'The LORD be exalted, who delights in the well-being of his servant'" (Psalm 35:27).

RESPONSE

Father God, give me a heart of thanksgiving. Grant me a pure heart with pure motives. May I always delight in the well-being of your servants. Amen.

YOUR TURN

Are you exalting yourself at the expense of others? If so, take some time to repent. Do your best to repair the damaged relationships that result from such behavior.

DAY 81: IS SELF-FLATTERY OUR WORST ENEMY?

TODAY'S READING: PSALM 36:1–4

KEY VERSE: PSALM 36:2

In their own eyes they flatter themselves too much to detect or hate their sin.

REFLECTION

Psalm 36 is a psalm of contrasts. David compares the wickedness of man with the amazing goodness of God. This opening portion of Psalm 36 touches only on the depravity of man. The picture we see of ourselves is not particularly flattering.

According to David, the problem begins with our eyes. He states, "There is no fear of God before their eyes. In their own eyes they flatter themselves too much to detect or hate their sin" (vv. 1–2).

The sinful person has a vision problem. He cannot see the dire consequences of his sin. Sin exacts a terrible price. Consider the lives wrecked by addiction to alcohol, drugs, or pornography. Furthermore, the damage is not limited to those caught in the terrible grip of sin. It overflows and contaminates all those around. Sin blinds the eyes so we cannot see the suffering we are causing to ourselves and others.

Over time, even so called "small" sins can exact a heavy toll on our lives. Often, in subtle ways, sin robs us of intimacy, peace, and joy. While we are blind to the problem, sin interferes with our relationship with God and those who are near to us. Daily, we should ask ourselves, do I have the right view of myself? In my mind, am I flattering myself too much to detect or hate my sin? Have I become blind to my faults—faults that may be obvious to others?

There is a biblical prescription for the blindness caused by our sinful condition. "The fear of the LORD is the beginning of wisdom; all who follow his precepts have good understanding" (Psalm 111:10). The fear of the Lord opens our eyes. The fear of the Lord leads to repentance, and the fear of the Lord enlightens our understanding.

What is keeping you from intimacy, joy, and peace today? Is it a plethora of secret sins that blind and bind you into unhealthy patterns of thinking? Ask God to give you a right view—an unflattering view of yourself—so that, with his help, you can change.

RESPONSE

Lord God, help me to see a true picture of myself. If I see sin in my life, help me to change. Grant me the gift of repentance through Jesus, who loved me to the point of death on a cross. Amen.

YOUR TURN

In our minds, all of us flatter ourselves. How do you maintain a right picture of yourself?

DAY 82: ARE YOU DRINKING FROM THE RIVER OF DELIGHTS?

TODAY'S READING: PSALM 36:5–9

KEY VERSE: PSALM 36:8

They feast on the abundance of your house;
you give them drink from your river of delights.

REFLECTION

As mentioned in my previous devotions, Psalm 36 is a psalm of contrasts. David compares the wickedness of man with the amazing goodness of God. The opening portion of Psalm 36 touches on the depravity of man. In today's reading, we behold the awesome love and kindness of God.

"Your love, LORD, reaches to the heavens, your faithfulness to the skies. Your righteousness is like the highest mountains, your justice like the great deep" (vv. 5–6a). The beautiful poetry of those words sends me off on a Rocky Mountain high.

God's love is reflected in the beauty of his creation. He nestled us into a world of incredible beauty and variety. From the grandeur of the mountains to the minute sea fauna, God is there—sustaining all—reigning over all. "You, LORD, preserve both people and animals. How priceless is your unfailing love, O God!" (vv. 6b–7a).

God's unfailing love stands in sharp contrast to man's rapacious capacity for hate and destruction. We glory in war, death, and bloodshed as though these are great accomplishments, when, in fact, they are a failure in love and forgiveness—the attributes of God. Yet, despite these failures, God showers us with his love and goodness. "People take refuge in the shadow of your wings. They feast on the abundance of your house; you give them drink from your river of delights" (vv. 7–8).

God is the source of the river of delights. Just as any good father enjoys bringing pleasure to his children, so, too, our heavenly Father delights in bringing joy to us. He is not stingy in his love, but overflowing with generosity, in many cases providing more than we can handle.

"For with you is the fountain of life; in your light we see light" (v. 9). The Lord is the author and source of all life. "God saw all that he had made, and it was very good. And there was evening, and there was morning—the sixth day" (Genesis 1:31). Only in him and through him do we see the light of day and the light of life. To God be praise forevermore!

RESPONSE

Lord God, thank you, thank you, thank you for your great love and faithfulness to me. Let your light shine in me and through me today. In the wonderful name of Jesus, I pray. Amen.

YOUR TURN

Have you been drinking from God's river of delights? List some things that bring you God-given joy.

DAY 83: DO YOU KNOW GOD?

TODAY'S READING: PSALM 36:10–12

KEY VERSE: PSALM 36:10

Continue your love to those who know you, your righteousness to the upright in heart.

REFLECTION

Do you know God? Are you well acquainted with God and his ways? Are you in regular conversation with him? I ask these questions because in this concluding portion of Psalm 36, David prays, "Continue your love to those who know you, your righteousness to the upright in heart."

Knowing God is or should be the great quest of our lives. This is our *raison d'etre*—our reason for being. We were created to know and love God. The Garden of Eden was first and foremost a place of communion with God. Yet, so often, we see ourselves running from God, or ignoring his invitation to draw close.

Jesus gives us this warning, "Not everyone who says to me, 'Lord, Lord,' will enter the kingdom of heaven, but only the one who does the will of my Father who is in heaven. Many will say to me on that day, 'Lord, Lord, did we not prophesy in your name and in your name drive out demons and in your name perform many miracles?' Then I will tell them plainly, 'I never knew you. Away from me, you evildoers!'" (Matthew 7:21–23).

From Christ's statement here, there appear to be two requirements for entering the Kingdom of Heaven: doing the will of the Father and knowing Jesus. I would argue that truly knowing Jesus helps us to discover and do the will of the Father. If you know someone really well, you know what they want—what will please them—without even asking. We need to aim for that kind of intimacy with God.

We come to know the mind of God because we have drawn close to the heart of God through time spent with him. Two-way prayer and meditation on his Word acquaints us with God's will and his ways—ways that do not change according to the whim of man.

God is not impressed by our prophetic or miraculous powers. He is not impressed by our power over demons. These, after all, are gifts from him. God is impressed by our obedience as we seek his face and do his will.

Our God is faithful. He will continue his love to those who know him. His righteousness will constantly flow to the upright in heart.

RESPONSE

Lord God, give me a humble heart that seeks after you. Show me your ways, O Lord. Give me a hunger for your Word. I want to know you more and more. Help me to do the Father's will today. I pray in the name of Jesus. Amen.

YOUR TURN

How do you get to know God better? What practices or activities grow your faith and knowledge of God?

DAY 84: RECEIVING THE DESIRES OF YOUR HEART

TODAY'S READING: PSALM 37:1–6

KEY VERSE: PSALM 37:4

Take delight in the LORD, and he will give you the desires of your heart.

REFLECTION

What are the desires of your heart? What do you want more than anything else? Wealth? Fame? Power and influence? We all have desires. Some are noble, some are not. How we manage and direct our desires fundamentally determines the direction of our lives.

Here in Psalm 37, David compares and contrasts the life of the evil person with the life of the individual who does right in God's eyes. The differences are stark. This is a night and day comparison. At its core, everything in life centers on the desires of our heart and how we handle them.

There is a promise embedded in this psalm. "Take delight in the LORD, and he will give you the desires of your heart." It's a promise that is well worth pondering.

Will the Lord grant us our desires if our desires are evil? Most certainly not! In Psalm 34 we read, "The face of the LORD is against those who do evil, to blot out their name from the earth" (v. 16).

God's promises are conditional. There is something required of us before the promise can take effect. In this case we are to "Take delight in the LORD." What does that really mean?

If I take delight in someone, my wife for example, I enjoy being around her. It's a delight to spend time with her. I take pleasure in the sound of her voice. I pay careful attention to her wishes and desires. Ah, there's that word again, desires. If I take delight in the Lord, then my desires will align themselves with the Lord's desires. I'll be concerned about what he wants. My selfish desires will be tempered by my love for him. He, in turn, will grant the desires of my heart because I love him and want the best for him and his eternal kingdom.

It's easy to get the desires of your heart, if your desires are his desires.

RESPONSE

Lord God, help me to delight myself in you. May I love what you love. Help me to recognize when my desires are right and wholesome, and when they are misdirected. I pray in the name of Jesus. Amen.

YOUR TURN

How do you keep your desires in check and in line with God?

DAY 85: WAITING FOR THE LORD

TODAY'S READING: PSALM 37:7–11

KEY VERSES: PSALM 37:7A, 8B

Be still before the LORD and wait patiently for
him; do not fret—it leads only to evil.

REFLECTION

When I consider this passage from Psalm 37, two verses
stand out: "Be still before the LORD and wait patiently for
him" and "do not fret—it leads only to evil."

My natural tendency is not to wait or be still. I tend to
fret and worry and then charge ahead simultaneously in
different directions. Trust me, it's hard to go in different
directions at the same time. The result is usually a bad
case of self-inflicted paralysis, which often results in—you
guessed it—a renewed bout of fret and worry. When will I
learn? When will we all learn?

Being still before the Lord requires practice. Being still
is a learned response, not a natural reaction. When we
wait for the Lord, we show that we trust him. We know that
he has not forgotten us or the problems we face. In every
situation, he has our best interests in mind, even if we
don't understand the reasons, causes, or solutions to our
difficulties.

By being still and waiting before the Lord, we demonstrate
we don't have the answer within ourselves. The answer—the
solution—lies only in him. If we wait patiently, he will show
us the way. And having waited patiently for him, we can

move forward with confidence when he gives us the green light.

I believe Jesus had the words of this psalm in mind when he gave these instructions in his Sermon on the Mount: "Therefore I tell you, do not worry about your life, what you will eat or drink; or about your body, what you will wear. Is not life more than food, and the body more than clothes? Look at the birds of the air; they do not sow or reap or store away in barns, and yet your heavenly Father feeds them. Are you not much more valuable than they? Can any one of you by worrying add a single hour to your life?" (Matthew 6:25–27).

We are to live in quiet confidence. In this psalm, we read this promise, "But the meek will inherit the land and enjoy peace and prosperity" (Psalm 37:11). We can put our trust in the God who stands behind that promise.

RESPONSE

Lord God, help me to trust you today. Give me a peaceful heart that I may wait patiently for you, even when the storms of life descend. In the name of Jesus, I pray. Amen.

YOUR TURN

Do you tend to fret? How might quiet prayer still your worries?

DAY 86: WHO IS UPHOLDING YOU?

TODAY'S READING: PSALM 37:12–17

KEY VERSE: PSALM 37:17

For the power of the wicked will be broken, but the LORD upholds the righteous.

REFLECTION

As previously stated, this psalm is a stark night and day comparison of the life of the evil person with the life of the individual who does right in God's eyes. The contrast is profound.

I cannot read the passages above without thinking of the evil that is loose in the world today. In Canada, in recent years, we had the trial of Luka Magnotta for his slaying of Jun Lin, a Chinese-born university student. Magnotta posted his killing of Lin with an icepick on YouTube. After dismembering his body, Magnotta mailed various body parts to schools and political party headquarters.

In Iraq and Syria, ISIS militants defiantly beheaded journalists and international aid workers in a cowardly display of their depravity. Those who hold different religious views have been executed, their women raped, and their children enslaved. We live in a wicked world where hatred and evil are trumpeted as worthy pursuits—pursuits that attract adoring young fanatics.

Verses twelve and fourteen of this psalm are as true today as when they were written three thousand years ago. "The wicked plot against the righteous and gnash their teeth at them," and "The wicked draw the sword and bend the bow to bring down the poor and needy, to slay those whose ways are upright."

The sin process is still at work in the hearts of men. "When tempted, no one should say, 'God is tempting me.' For God cannot be tempted by evil, nor does he tempt anyone; but each person is tempted when they are dragged away by their own evil desire and enticed. Then, after desire has conceived, it gives birth to sin; and sin, when it is full-grown, gives birth to death" (James 1:13–15).

But thanks be to God. We have this promise, "for the power of the wicked will be broken, but the LORD upholds the righteous" (Psalm 37:17). God will uphold us as we put our trust in him.

RESPONSE

Lord God, you are my upholder—my help in evil times, in times of trouble. I put my trust in you. Hold me in the palm of your hand. I pray in the name of Jesus. Amen.

YOUR TURN

How do you fight evil? Where does evil start? We must examine our hearts.

DAY 87: GIVERS AND TAKERS

TODAY'S READING: PSALM 37:18–22

KEY VERSE: PSALM 37:21

The wicked borrow and do not repay, but the righteous give generously

REFLECTION

I have heard it said that there are two kinds of people in the world—givers and takers. Notice, I didn't say givers and receivers. We all are receivers from the first breath we take, as we receive love and nourishment from our mothers. But there is a subtle, but important difference between receiving and taking. The receiver takes what is freely offered. The taker takes regardless if it is offered or not.

Takers feel the world owes them something. Givers owe a debt of love and make regular payments on that debt. The apostle Paul urges us, "Owe no one anything except to love one another, for he who loves another has fulfilled the law" (Romans 13:8 NKJV).

Here in Psalm 37, David declares, "The wicked borrow and do not repay, but the righteous give generously" (v. 21). There is something counterintuitive about generosity. Generosity breeds prosperity, whereas hoarding leads to poverty. "One person gives freely, yet gains even more; another withholds unduly, but comes to poverty. A generous person will prosper; whoever refreshes others will be refreshed" (Proverbs 11:24–25).

Why is this the case? Job gives us this nugget of wisdom, "Anyone who withholds kindness from a friend forsakes the fear of the Almighty" (Job 6:14). The Almighty oversees our lives. He sees when we withhold kindness from a friend, and he sees when we give generously. "He is a rewarder of those who diligently seek Him" (Hebrews 11:6b NKJV).

A generous spirit reflects the Spirit of God, who freely gives us all things, including his Son. His Son generously gave his life for our redemption, and for the forgiveness of our sins. Forgiveness is freely offered and is free for the taking from a lavishly generous God. Have you received what he offers?

Our amazing God turns takers into givers. Saul of Tarsus was a taker, but when he encountered Jesus on the road to Damascus, he became a giver—a forgiven giver (Acts 9). Saul became Paul. Hate turned to love. Taking from the world turned to giving.

RESPONSE

Lord God, turn me around. Help me to be generous with those in need. You gave so much to me. Now help me be a giver—a reflection of you in the world. I pray in the name of Jesus. Amen.

YOUR TURN

Can we give without receiving? Which comes first?

DAY 88: WHO DELIGHTS YOUR HEART?

TODAY'S READING: PSALM 37:23–20

KEY VERSE: PSALM 37:23

The LORD makes firm the steps of the one who delights in him.

REFLECTION

According to Psalm 37, there is a string of blessings bequeathed to the righteous. We are kept safe—held secure in the palm of God's hand. Furthermore, these blessings are intergenerational. The children of the righteous are blessed, so they can be a blessing to their parents and others.

As parents and grandparents can attest, children can be a great blessing, or if they are corrupted by rebellion and disobedience, they can become a curse, making life difficult for all around them.

Much of the trouble in the world today is self-inflicted. By choosing the path of anger, selfishness, and resentment, we heap sorrow on our own heads. Conversely, if we choose to follow the Lord along the path of love, generosity, and forgiveness, we set ourselves up to receive blessings from our heavenly Father.

Through the ages, David's admonition rings true. "Turn from evil and do good; then you will dwell in the land forever" (v. 27).

But God's blessings rest on the premise found in verse 23: "The LORD makes firm the steps of the one who delights in him."

The questions we need to continually ask ourselves are, "Am I delighting myself in the Lord? Is he my chief joy in life? Do I hunger for his Word and his presence in my life?"

RESPONSE

Lord God, help me to delight myself in you. May I love what you love. Help me to position myself to receive your blessings. I pray in your Son's name. Amen.

YOUR TURN

Are you living proof of God's intergenerational blessing on those who delight in him? When do you long for times of sweet communion with Jesus?

DAY 89: WHAT IS YOUR INTENTION?

TODAY'S READING: PSALM 37:30–34

KEY VERSES: PSALM 37:30–31

The mouths of the righteous utter wisdom, and their tongues speak what is just. The law of their God is in their hearts; their feet do not slip.

REFLECTION

A few years ago, in Canada's capital, we saw aspects of Psalm 37 play out in real time. A terrorist, with planned intent, gunned down Corporal Nathan Cirillo while he stood guard before the National War Memorial. This cowardly act highlighted the contempt of those who celebrate evil toward those who stand for righteousness, truth, and justice. The contrast between those who love peace and those who revel in violence is stark indeed.

"The mouths of the righteous utter wisdom, and their tongues speak what is just. The law of their God is in their hearts; their feet do not slip" (v. 30) versus "The wicked lie in wait for the righteous, intent on putting them to death" (v. 32).

When evil raises its brutal head, we need not be intimidated. We need to take heart. When we stand on the side of truth, justice, and love, we do not stand alone. God is with us. He is on our side. He has our back. As the psalmist declares, we need to "Hope in the LORD and keep his way" (v. 34).

The way of the Lord is the way of love. Jesus said to his disciples, "No one has greater love than this—that one lays down his life for his friends" (John 15:13 NET). Jesus went on to demonstrate that supreme love by laying down his life on the cross for our redemption.

The questions we need to continually ask ourselves are, "What is my motivation? Am I motivated by love or am I driven by hate? Am I drawing close to the God of love and hope? Is my life a demonstration of God's redeeming love, or am I only concerned about my selfish interests?"

Corporal Nathan Cirillo laid down his life in the service of his country. Which god will you serve? Will you serve the god of self, or the selfless God—the God whose hands were pierced for you? The choice is yours.

RESPONSE

Lord God, we live in a very troubled world. When evil rises, we put our trust in you. Help me to walk in the way of love. Surround me with your peace. Keep those who serve their country safe. I pray in the name of Jesus. Amen.

YOUR TURN

How can you honor those who lay down their lives in the service of their country? What makes their sacrifice special for you?

DAY 90: SALVATION COMES FROM THE LORD

TODAY'S READING: PSALM 37:35–40

KEY VERSE: PSALM 37:39

The salvation of the righteous comes from the LORD; he is their stronghold in time of trouble.

REFLECTION

Today's reading is the concluding portion of Psalm 37. As noted previously, this entire Psalm contrasts the life of the righteous person with the individual who pursues a life of sin and illicit gain. The righteous will receive their reward and the man who does evil will be destroyed.

We all reap what we sow. If we sow seeds of selfishness, hate, and discord, we will reap a harvest of ruin. Paul, the apostle, gives us this warning, "Do not be deceived: God cannot be mocked. A man reaps what he sows. Whoever sows to please their flesh, from the flesh will reap destruction; whoever sows to please the Spirit, from the Spirit will reap eternal life" (Galatians 6:7–8).

We can readily conclude the good man will live because of his goodness. In other words, the righteous person will be saved because of his righteous deeds. But that's not what Psalm 37 teaches. In fact, the idea that one is saved because of one's righteousness runs contrary to the message of this psalm and the entire counsel of Holy Scripture. The psalmist clearly states, "The salvation of the righteous comes from the LORD" (Psalm 37:39).

We are not saved by our righteousness. We are saved by the Lord. It is because of his great mercy that we are saved. This aligns with New Testament teaching as Paul declares, "For it is by grace you have been saved, through faith—and this is not from yourselves, it is the gift of God—not by works, so that no one can boast" (Ephesians 2:8–9).

Yes, we are called to live righteous lives and to do good works, but let's not deceive ourselves. We will not earn our way to heaven. Jesus is the only way to heaven. Our feeble efforts won't take us very far. We need God's forgiveness and the power of his redeeming blood. We are saved because we take refuge in him.

RESPONSE

Lord God, I thank you for Jesus. I am thankful I can put my complete trust in you. I am saved by your amazing grace not by my effort. Hallelujah! Lord Jesus, you are "the way, the truth and the life" (John 14:6). Amen.

YOUR TURN

When have you relied on your righteousness rather than God's grace? How can you develop a greater appreciation for God's grace and acceptance?

DAY 91: LAMENTING OVER SIN

Today's Reading: Psalm 38:1–8

Key Verse: Psalm 38:4

My guilt has overwhelmed me like a burden too heavy to bear.

REFLECTION

Psalm 38 is a psalm of personal lamentation. The psalmist, David, laments the state of his personal and spiritual health. Notes of joy and triumph are absent from this psalm. Instead, we find David in a state of deep melancholy.

What is the cause of this melancholy—this depression verging on despair? David attributes his current ill health to sin. He has sinned and is bearing the consequences of his sin. His words of confession make this perfectly clear. "Because of your wrath there is no health in my body; there is no soundness in my bones because of my sin. My guilt has overwhelmed me like a burden too heavy to bear" (vv. 3–4).

What a refreshingly different approach to one's problems. Rather than blaming others or blaming God, David takes responsibility for his self-inflicted difficulties. How different from the pop psychology of today. Rather than deal with the sin issue, we are often advised to pop a pill, blame a parent, a colleague, or society in general. Rather than take our problems to God, the world encourages us to indulge ourselves with another bottle, another doughnut, or another spouse. Meanwhile, our putrid load of sin piles ever higher.

David was on the right track when he confessed his sin to the Lord. He laments, "My wounds fester and are loathsome because of my sinful folly" (v. 5).

Thanks be to God! He can handle our sinful folly. He sent Jesus to die on the cross to wipe away our sins. Healing, forgiveness, and redemption are available through the blood Jesus shed.

RESPONSE

Lord God, I thank you for Jesus. I am thankful I can put my complete trust in you. You forgive me and cleanse me from all my sins. I am saved by your amazing grace not by my effort. Amen.

YOUR TURN

When was the last time you truly lamented over sin in your life?

DAY 92: THE LORD SEES AND HEARS

TODAY'S READING: PSALM 38:9–16

KEY VERSE: PSALM 38:9

All my longings lie open before you, LORD; my sighing is not hidden from you.

REFLECTION

Here in Psalm 38, David has brought all his troubles before the Lord. He laments over his sin and the downcast state in which he finds himself. Hear his confession, "All my longings lie open before you, LORD; my sighing is not hidden from you. My heart pounds, my strength fails me; even the light has gone from my eyes" (vv. 9–10).

In humble prayer, David has come before a God who always hears and sees. God hears and sees even when we wish he could not. He sees our triumphs and our failures, our victories over temptation, and our slide into defeat. He hears every idle word and understands every crass and selfish thought. The Lord sees and hears. He saw Adam's sin in the Garden before he met with him in the cool of the evening. God sees our sins long before we bow in repentance.

God sees and hears all we say and do. This should bring comfort to the soul in distress and a healthy fear to the soul tempted to sin. "All my longings lie open before you, LORD"—the wholesome longings and those that spring from impure motives. The Lord sees my needs and my wants, my hopes and my dreams, but, more than that, God understands my motives. David brought all of this before the Lord, and so should we.

Though we may not see the pain of those around us, God sees our suffering. Though we may be deaf to the needs of others, God is not deaf to our plea for help. Though we may stand mute when others need defense or encouragement, our God speaks. He does not remain silent. His Spirit speaks even to you—even to me.

RESPONSE

Lord God, speak to me when I am downcast. Lift me when I am in need. Forgive me when I fail. You are my help and my strength. "LORD, I wait for you; you will answer, Lord my God" (v. 15). Amen.

YOUR TURN

How has the all-hearing, all-seeing God helped you? Take a moment to reflect on how the Lord has helped you in the past.

DAY 93: ARE YOU TROUBLED BY SIN?

Today's Reading: Psalm 38:17–22

Key Verse: Psalm 38:18

I confess my iniquity; I am troubled by my sin.

Reflection

Today's reading is the concluding portion of Psalm 38. As noted previously, this entire Psalm is a lament over sin, and the trouble and affliction it has brought into David's life. Rather than blaming others or blaming God, David takes responsibility for his self-inflicted difficulties. In anguish of spirit, he cries out, "I confess my iniquity; I am troubled by my sin."

Are you troubled by your sin, or do you revel in it? Have the consequences of sin started to bite? The writer of the book of Hebrews tells us that Moses "chose to be mistreated along with the people of God rather than to enjoy the fleeting pleasures of sin" (Hebrews 11:25). There are pleasures in sin for a season, but the long-term consequences are pain and death. It would appear from a full reading of Psalm 38 that David is suffering some of the consequences of his misguided sin.

However, David has the correct response. He confesses his sin and throws himself upon the mercies of God. Hear his humble plea, "LORD, do not forsake me; do not be far from me, my God. Come quickly to help me, my Lord and my Savior" (Psalm 38:21–22).

God's ears are always open to that kind of prayer. We may believe we have fallen too far—our sin is too great, or we have sunk too low. But God hears our cry and his grace is sufficient. His mercy knows no bounds. The blood of Christ flows to the lowest valley. He can cleanse the vilest heart if we call out to him.

Repentance is a wonderful gift, perhaps the greatest gift of all. At various times in his life, David fell into the grip of sin. But David knew how to repent, and as a result, found favor in the eyes of God. Discover the gift of repentance today. It's more than feeling sorry for yourself. It's a one-eighty-degree turn from pursuing sin to pursuing God.

RESPONSE

Lord God, grant me the gift of repentance. I am thankful Jesus died on the cross to wash me clean. Hallelujah! I want to pursue you, Lord. You are my help and my righteousness. My salvation comes from you. Amen.

YOUR TURN

Are you troubled by sin? Have you found a remedy?

DAY 94: THE DILEMMA OF SILENCE

TODAY'S READING: PSALM 39:1–5

KEY VERSE: PSALM 39:3

My heart grew hot within me. While I meditated, the fire burned; then I spoke with my tongue.

REFLECTION

Do you often find yourself in a dilemma of silence? In this psalm, David finds himself in this very predicament. He decided, "I will put a muzzle on my mouth while in the presence of the wicked" (v. 1).

If your ways and your thoughts run contrary to the ways of the wicked, you are in good company. You are in the company of the Lord. But don't be surprised if you are socially ostracized when you express your opinion. The ungodly rarely want to hear about the error of their ways. They usually prefer to blunder along in the darkness and curse the sudden appearance of light. Exposure is seen as too great a threat to their way of life.

David remained silent, "not even saying anything good" (v. 2). But it was an uneasy silence.

Often, as I listen to news reports and the ruminations of cultural icons, I find myself in an uneasy silence. We live in a world that has largely abandoned God and his ways. When we embrace the God of the Bible, we are choosing to swim upstream against the flow of gravity and humanity. The world heaps scorn on those who have caught a different vision.

In his silence, David's anguish increased. He states, "My heart grew hot within me. While I meditated, the fire burned" (v. 3).

Is passion for God burning in your heart? True worth and eternal values can only be found in him.

RESPONSE

Lord, show me your ways. Show me how much I need you day by day. Help me to value every day you give me on this earth. Shine your light in me and through me by the power of Jesus. Amen.

YOUR TURN

Are we silent too often when we should speak? Reflect on times when you have spoken up and good has resulted.

DAY 95: SURELY EVERYONE IS BUT A BREATH

Today's Reading: Psalm 39:6–13

Key Verse: Psalm 39:7–8

But now, LORD, what do I look for? My hope is in you. Save me from all my transgressions.

REFLECTION

Today, we conclude Psalm 39. Here, we find David in a silent, reflective mood. He contemplates the brevity of life and the certainty of the grave. In yesterday's psalm reading, he prayed, "Show me, LORD, my life's end and the number of my days; let me know how fleeting my life is" (Psalm 39:4).

Why would knowing the number of our days matter? Well, knowing the number of our days should focus our minds on making the most of the time available to us. Our days on this earth are not infinite. We are each allotted a predetermined number of days. In Psalm 139, verse 16, another psalm attributed to David, we read, "Your eyes saw my unformed body; all the days ordained for me were written in your book before one of them came to be."

We have no control, or at best, limited control over the number of days we live on this earth. But how and with whom we spend those days is within the range of our effective will. I can break my marital vows and my wife's heart, or I can be true to her and my words spoken before God. I can love and raise my children in godly discipline, or I can neglect them, or alienate them, through anger or harsh punishment. I can be faithful to my Redeemer or I can turn my back on him. These are decisions that fall within the scope of my will. In this life and the next, I will be accountable for the decisions I make. Undoubtedly, this is why David cries out, "But now, LORD, what do I look for? My hope is in you. Save me from all my transgressions" (Psalm 39:7–8).

RESPONSE

Lord God, I need your saving help. Through the redemptive blood of Jesus, keep me from being trapped and controlled by my transgressions. I need your presence in my life so that I can make the most of my days. May your kingdom rule extend to me and through me to others. Amen.

YOUR TURN

How would you live your life differently if you knew how many days you had left? What priorities would change?

DAY 96: THE LORD WHO LIFTS

TODAY'S READING: PSALM 40:1–5

KEY VERSE: PSALM 40:2

He lifted me out of the slimy pit, out of the mud and mire; he set my feet on a rock and gave me a firm place to stand.

REFLECTION

Psalm 40 begins as a testimony of David. We do not know at which point in his life David penned this psalm, but we know David was speaking from personal experience. Many times, this shepherd of Israel "waited patiently for the LORD" (v. 1a). On numerous occasions, he cried out to the Lord. The remarkable truth is that despite all his troubles, David can testify the Lord "turned to me and heard my cry" (v. 1).

Is that your testimony too? Have you been rescued by the Lord? Has he heard your cry and lifted you "out of the slimy pit, out of the mud and mire"? I am continually amazed at how the Lord stoops down to the level of humanity. The high and lofty Lord of Hosts, seated in the heavens, stoops down to rescue the likes of you and me.

I don't deserve to be rescued. In most instances, the mud and the mire in which I am stuck is mud and mire I have produced. All too often, I fall into the slimy pit I have dug. Why should God rescue me? I have gotten myself into this mess. But when I call to him, the Lord hears my voice and stoops to rescue me. God rescued David three thousand years ago, and he is still rescuing us today. Two thousand years ago, God came to the city of David. He stepped into the mud and the mire of a Bethlehem stable. Jesus was born to lift us from the dung into heights of heaven. He came on a rescue mission that extends to you and me.

With David, I can testify, "Many, LORD my God, are the wonders you have done, the things you planned for us. None can compare with you; were I to speak and tell of your deeds, they would be too many to declare" (v. 5).

RESPONSE

Lord God, I thank you for Jesus. I am thankful I can put my complete trust in you. I am rescued by your amazing grace, not by my effort. When I fall, you lift me up. Hallelujah! Amen.

YOUR TURN

Take some time to reflect on occasions when God has rescued you. What emotions did you experience when God's help arrived?

DAY 97: ARE YOUR EARS OPEN?

TODAY'S READING: PSALM 40:6–10

KEY VERSES: PSALM 40:7–8

Then I said, "Here I am, I have come—it is written about me in the scroll. I desire to do your will, my God; your law is within my heart."

REFLECTION

The first half of today's Psalm reading is quoted directly in Hebrews 10:5–7. The writer of the book of Hebrews saw Jesus as the prophetic fulfillment of this passage. When God came to earth in bodily form as the Babe of Bethlehem, he came clothed in humanity. Jesus came with his ears wide open to the voice of his heavenly Father. He came to do his Father's will. For Jesus, the Father's will meant going to the whipping post and climbing the hill of Golgotha to die in agony on the cross. Jesus became the necessary sacrifice for the sins of the world—the sacrifice the Father desired.

Has God opened your ears to his voice? Have you loved God until it hurt? It hurt Jesus to do his Father's will. If we are disciples of Jesus, should we expect better treatment than our Master? Often, what we hear preached is a sugar-coated gospel that asks little of us. Yet Jesus asked his disciples for their lives. He said, "Anyone who loves their father or mother more than me is not worthy of me; anyone who loves their son or daughter more than me is not worthy of me. Whoever does not take up their cross and follow me is not worthy of me. Whoever finds their life will lose it, and whoever loses their life for my sake will find it" (Matthew 10:37–39).

Have you lost your life for the sake of Jesus? Now, that's a high calling with a steep price attached. Are your ears open to God's calling? There are times when I don't want to hear God's voice. That's why I don't seek him in prayer. He may tell me something I don't want to hear. All too often, I am his reluctant servant. I would rather do my will than his. God must change my desires. My desires must become his desires. Only then can I serve with joy. Our Savior's desire was always to do his Father's will. From an early age he was about his Father's business, fulfilling his Father's plan for his life. Whose plan are you following?

RESPONSE

Lord God, help me to truly hear and obey your voice. I want to be your disciple, Lord Jesus. Thank you for your great sacrifice by which you purchased my redemption. Amen.

YOUR TURN

Have you heard God's voice and walked away? He doesn't give up easily. He remains faithful. He renews his call on our lives.

DAY 98: SAVING GRACE FOR THE DAYS AHEAD

TODAY'S READING: PSALM 40:11–17

KEY VERSE: PSALM 40:13

Be pleased to save me, LORD; come quickly, LORD, to help me.

REFLECTION

David begins Psalm 40 by praising the Lord for rescuing him from the slimy pit of the past. But David ends this psalm with a fresh appeal for God's mercy. "Do not withhold your mercy from me, LORD; may your love and faithfulness always protect me" (v. 11).

As we move forward, it is only fitting that we take time to praise God for what he has done for us in the past. Let us never forget the Lord's faithfulness has brought us to this point. We are not where we are today because of our own cleverness, effort, or ability. Every talent we have is a gift from God. Every breath we take is a gift from the Giver of Life.

Yet again, David appeals for God's assistance. "Be pleased to save me, LORD; come quickly, LORD, to help me" (v. 13).

By the grace of God, I have experienced an initial point of salvation, but to maintain a flourishing relationship, I need to experience fresh surges of God's grace and love. Grace (*charis*) in the full New Testament sense means much more than just unmerited favor. It means we are recipients of God's providential gifting and power to live a maximized life under his caring guidance. There's something supernatural about grace. It goes beyond human ability or ingenuity because it comes from the Lord, the Maker of heaven and earth. When we call out to God as David did, we are tapping into an ocean full of help, strength, and possibilities beyond fathoming.

May that grace, that charis of God, be with you and upon you in the days ahead.

RESPONSE

Lord God, I need you as I face the days ahead. Equip me with divine grace and ability for each day through the love and power of Jesus. Amen.

YOUR TURN

Describe or journal how you have experienced God's grace in the past week—the past year.

DAY 99: REGARD FOR THE WEAK

TODAY'S READING: PSALM 41:1-6

KEY VERSE: PSALM 41:1

Blessed are those who have regard for the weak;
the LORD delivers them in times of trouble.

REFLECTION

Psalm 41 reminds us compassion and empathy are at the core of what it means to be a follower of the Lord. David begins this psalm with this declaration, "Blessed are those who have regard for the weak."

Social justice and care for the poor are not small matters in eyes of Lord. Ancient Israel was destroyed and sent into exile because of their disregard for the poor. "The LORD enters into judgment against the elders and leaders of his people: 'It is you who have ruined my vineyard; the plunder from the poor is in your houses. What do you mean by crushing my people and grinding the faces of the poor?' declares the LORD, the LORD Almighty" (Isaiah 3:14-15).

Why is regard for the weak so pivotal in having a right relationship with God? Lack of care or empathy for the needy is based on a kind of self-deception. We see ourselves as better than those who are weak or needy. Yet if we examine ourselves, we have all gone through times when we were weak and needy. Sometimes, we may need a reminder that our current state of self-sufficiency can come to an end in a moment.

This morning, I very nearly hit a pedestrian as she rushed across the street. I sounded my horn thinking she was in error. A quick glance showed she was crossing with the walk light, and I had completely missed a red light. Oops! Turns out, I was the one in need of correction and forgiveness. My smug self-assurance needed a quick correction.

Are you doing well now? Praise God. The day will come when you need God's help and protection. Do you see someone in need? Help as you are able. The day will come when you will need the help and forgiveness you have offered others.

RESPONSE

Lord God, forgive me when I have looked down on others in need. Open my eyes to someone I may help today. In Christ's name I pray. Amen.

YOUR TURN

How do you keep yourself from the deception of pride? How open are you to correction?

DAY 100: FROM BETRAYAL TO TRIUMPH

TODAY'S READING: PSALM 41:7–13

KEY VERSE: PSALM 41:9

Even my close friend, someone I trusted, one who shared my bread, has turned against me.

REFLECTION

This concluding portion of Psalm 41 comes with a prophetic twist. As Jesus sat with his disciples at the Last Supper, he said he was fulfilling the words of this psalm.

"'I am not referring to all of you; I know those I have chosen. But this is to fulfill this passage of Scripture: "He who shared my bread has turned against me." I am telling you now before it happens, so that when it does happen you will believe that I am who I am. Very truly I tell you, whoever accepts anyone I send accepts me; and whoever accepts me accepts the one who sent me.'

"After he had said this, Jesus was troubled in spirit and testified, 'Very truly I tell you, one of you is going to betray me'" (John 13:18–21).

David experienced the heartbreak of betrayal. Not only did David's friends turn on him, but his own son, Absalom, sought to snatch the throne in a bloody coup—an act of open rebellion (see 2 Samuel 15–18).

David was betrayed by his son, Absalom. Jesus was betrayed by his friend and disciple, Judas Iscariot. Both men, however, stayed loyal to God the Father. Jesus willingly went to the cross when he could have resisted arrest. He rebuked Peter for using his sword. "'Put your sword back in its place,' Jesus said to him, 'for all who draw the sword will die by the sword. Do you think I cannot call on my Father, and he will at once put at my disposal more than twelve legions of angels?'" (Matthew 26:52–53).

Jesus experienced the resurrection truth of David's words. "Because of my integrity you uphold me and set me in your presence forever. Praise be to the LORD, the God of Israel, from everlasting to everlasting. Amen and Amen" (Psalm 41:12–13).

RESPONSE

Lord, I thank you for Jesus. Through Jesus, I can overcome all things, even betrayal. Amen.

YOUR TURN

Have you experienced betrayal? How has the Lord upheld your cause?

DAY 101: ARE YOU THIRSTY FOR THE LORD?

TODAY'S READING: PSALM 42:1–5

KEY VERSE: PSALM 42:2

My soul thirsts for God, for the living God. When can I go and meet with God?

REFLECTION

Thirst is one of our most basic cravings. Our need for water far exceeds our need for food. The human body can go sixty days or more without food, but only about ten days without water. Your body needs water because it's comprised mostly of water. About two thirds of your body weight is water.

But you are more than skin filled with bones and water. The apostle Paul closes his first letter to the Thessalonians with this prayer, "May God himself, the God of peace, sanctify you through and through. May your whole spirit, soul and body be kept blameless at the coming of our Lord Jesus Christ" (1 Thessalonians 5:23).

As Paul states, we are spirit, soul, and body. By nature—by God's design—you are two-thirds spiritual. You are more than a collection of molecules. You are a living soul with a spirit that was designed and intended to commune with God. Therefore, just as our physical body thirsts for water, so our spiritual man thirsts for God.

This should be our constant prayer, "As the deer pants for streams of water, so my soul pants for you, my God. My soul thirsts for God, for the living God. When can I go and meet with God?" (Psalm 42:1–2).

Are you thirsting for God? The truth is we all thirst for God. Some of us know how to mask our thirst, or we substitute other things for the true living water. But the thirst remains. We need to heed the invitation of Jesus. "On the last and greatest day of the festival, Jesus stood and said in a loud voice, 'Let anyone who is thirsty come to me and drink'" (John 7:37).

RESPONSE

Lord God, I thank you for Jesus. I am thankful that you are the true water of life and when we drink of your Spirit, springs of water flow from us. Hallelujah! Amen.

YOUR TURN

Have you tasted the life-changing, life-invigorating water of Christ? How do you quench your spiritual thirst?

DAY 102: HOPE FOR THE DOWNCAST SOUL

TODAY'S READING: PSALM 42:6–11

KEY VERSE: PSALM 42:11

Why, my soul, are you downcast? Why so disturbed within me? Put your hope in God, for I will yet praise him, my Savior and my God.

REFLECTION

Let's face the truth. We all go through times when we are downcast. In fact, just a few minutes ago, my wife asked me, "Are you grumpy today?"

I was surprised she'd noticed. I thought I had been hiding my downcast state quite well. After reflecting a moment, I answered, "I guess I am." Then I began to justify my grumpy mood. "It's cold, windy, and snowing. Again! And my face feels numb and puffy from my visit to the dentist."

What I didn't explain was the discouragement I felt about my writing career. My literary agent may drop me as a client. Book sales have been sluggish. Every news report I read seems to be filled with gloom and dire predictions. I have a backache, probably from shoveling snow. And did I mention this Canadian winter feels interminable? Along with the psalmist, David, I can say, "My soul is downcast within me" (v. 6).

However, David didn't stay wallowing in his pity party. He rallied through songs of worship and prayer. Hear his words, "By day the LORD directs his love, at night his song is with me—a prayer to the God of my life" (v. 8).

When I am discouraged—when you are discouraged—we can both do the same. We can turn to the Lord in song. I can pray to the God of my life—the God who knew me in my mother's womb—the God who left his throne to rescue me. Why should I be downcast when Jesus cast himself down on my behalf? He was cast down so that through faith in him, I will be lifted up.

Though discouragement comes to all, we also have a Savior who accepts us as we are. We can call on him during such times.

RESPONSE

Lord God, I thank you for Jesus. I am thankful he willingly laid down his life so that I could be forgiven and experience new life. I put my hope in my Savior and my God. Hallelujah! Amen.

YOUR TURN

What do you do during times of discouragement? How can you turn to the Lord for hope and encouragement?

DAY 103: HAVE YOU BEEN ALTERED AT THE ALTAR?

TODAY'S READING: PSALM 43

KEY VERSE: PSALM 43:4

Then I will go to the altar of God, to God, my joy and my delight. I will praise you with the lyre, O God, my God.

REFLECTION

I want to be proven right. Over and over again, I find myself pleading to be heard—pleading to be proven right. That's what it means to be vindicated. As I look about my country—as I look about the world—and read or watch the news of the day, I see so much injustice. Senseless death and destruction are everywhere.

Courts intended to protect the innocent and vulnerable do the complete opposite. Evil is on a rampage. Islamic militants taunt and behead the innocent. Russian tanks invade Ukraine as long range artillery flattens villages. Vicious rapists glory in their shame. In our cities, gangster thugs roam freely.

But there is a better way—the way of the cross—the way of the Prince of Peace. Why can't others see it? Why can't they grasp it? Along with David, we cry out, "Vindicate me, my God, and plead my cause against an unfaithful nation. Rescue me from those who are deceitful and wicked" (v. 1).

In this bleak state of affairs, David appeals to the mercy of the Lord, "Send me your light and your faithful care, let them lead me; let them bring me to your holy mountain, to the place where you dwell" (v. 3).

David journeys to the altar. He is altered at the altar. The world is altered at the altar of God. Vindication comes at the altar. Victories over sin are won at the altar. Jesus is the sacrifice on the altar of God, and when we gaze on him, we are changed. Jesus said, "Just as Moses lifted up the snake in the wilderness, so the Son of Man must be lifted up, that everyone who believes may have eternal life in him" (John 3:14–15). Because of the cross—the altar of God—we have hope for the future.

RESPONSE

Lord God, alter me at the foot of the cross. I need you to change my heart, my life, my attitude. I put my hope in you, Lord. You are my Savior and my God. Amen.

YOUR TURN

How has your life been altered by the cross? Reflect on how God has changed you.

DAY 104: WHAT BRINGS YOU SUCCESS?

TODAY'S READING: PSALM 44:1–8

KEY VERSE: PSALM 44:3

It was not by their sword that they won the land, nor did their arm bring them victory; it was your right hand, your arm, and the light of your face, for you loved them.

REFLECTION

What brings you success? There are thousands of books, blogs, and advice columns out there that promise you success. If you will just do this, that, and this other thing success is sure to come your way. Now, don't misunderstand me. Many of those self-improvement tips and success formulas can be helpful, if applied. And educating yourself on sound habits and business practices can be rewarding.

But if you do succeed, what is the source of your success? The author of Psalm 44 would respond by saying success does not come from a formula, a habit, or a tip. Success and victory come from the Lord. In this psalm, the psalmist refers to the conquest of Canaan by the children of Israel. "It was not by their sword that they won the land, nor did their arm bring them victory; it was your right hand, your arm, and the light of your face, for you loved them" (v. 3).

If you succeed in your field of endeavor, what will be the reason for your success? Undoubtedly, hard work, sound practices, wisdom, and creativity all play a part. There are plenty of people who have these character traits in spades, but still fail to reach their potential. We only succeed—succeed in the fullest sense—when God is working with us. The apostle Paul reminds us of this truth, "No, in all these things we are more than conquerors through him who loved us" (Romans 8:37).

We conquer in our field of endeavor when God is working with us. If you succeed, who is the reason for your success?

RESPONSE

Lord God, any success I have comes from you. Every triumph is a victory that you bring. Help me to always remember you are my source. I succeed because of your love, Lord Jesus. Amen.

YOUR TURN

What gifts, talents, or insights have you gained? Take a moment to give thanks to God for his help.

DAY 105: WHAT DO YOU DO IN TIMES OF DEFEAT?

TODAY'S READING: PSALM 44:9–16

KEY VERSE: PSALM 44:9

But now you have rejected and humbled us; you no longer go out with our armies.

REFLECTION

Psalm 44 begins on a very positive note as the psalmist recalls the goodness of the Lord and the great victories Israel has won because of the Lord's help. But that was the past. This is now, and the triumphs of bygone years are just fading memories. The current reality as described in this portion of the psalm is a depressing litany of disgrace, disaster, and defeat.

"But now you have rejected and humbled us; you no longer go out with our armies. You made us retreat before the enemy, and our adversaries have plundered us" (vv. 9–10).

After we turn our lives over to Christ, we can pretend everything will go well for us. Some things do. After all, isn't God on our side? Isn't he working on our behalf for our success? Why would God allow stress, trouble, and hardship to come our way?

The truth is the Lord is far more interested in developing our character than our comfort. Character development doesn't happen without adversity. James, our Lord's brother, offered some sound advice on this topic.

"Consider it pure joy, my brothers and sisters, whenever you face trials of many kinds, because you know that the testing of your faith produces perseverance. Let perseverance finish its work so that you may be mature and complete, not lacking anything" (James 1:2–4).

I dislike adversity, but we should greet adversity as a friend—a friend that provokes us to prayer and perseverance. Hard times push us into discovering God's grace afresh.

RESPONSE

Lord God, help me to see the difficulties I face as steppingstones to victory. I know I need your help, so I call out to you. Change me through the hard times. You are my Savior and my God. Amen.

YOUR TURN

How has adversity helped to develop your character?

DAY 106: POURING OUT YOUR COMPLAINT TO GOD

TODAY'S READING: PSALM 44:17–26

KEY VERSE: PSALM 44:17

All this came upon us, though we had not forgotten you; we had not been false to your covenant.

REFLECTION

As previously noted, Psalm 44 begins in a very positive fashion as the psalmist recalls the goodness of the Lord and the great victories Israel has won because of the Lord's help. But that is not the present reality. The present reality is filled with defeat, death, and destruction. The psalmist moves from rejoicing over past victories to lamenting over present-day tribulations. Hear his words of anguish, "Yet for your sake we face death all day long; we are considered as sheep to be slaughtered" (v. 22).

What do you do in the midst of defeat? Do you put on a brave face and pretend all is going well? There may be occasions when putting on a brave face is warranted, even necessary—but inside, when we are alone with our thoughts, we question why God would allow such things. Why would God allow a child to die? Why would he allow a natural disaster like an earthquake to claim countless innocent lives? Normally, these life-shattering matters don't come with pat answers in tow. We are left in a state of grief and bewilderment.

Often, believers see such events as retribution for sins committed against a holy God. But note the psalmist's complaint: "All this came upon us, though we had not forgotten you; we had not been false to your covenant. Our hearts had not turned back; our feet had not strayed from your path" (vv. 17–18).

The brutal truth is bad things happen to good people. Sometimes, Christians are martyred on a beach in Libya. Sometimes, a cruel disease hems us in on every side, and there is no escape, aside from death and heaven's door. Sometimes, all we can do is pour out our complaint before a God of unfailing love.

RESPONSE

Lord God, when life is hard, help me to remember to bring my complaints and travails to you. You are bigger than any agony or grief I may face. I call out to you, my Savior and my God. Amen.

YOUR TURN

Do you feel God been unfair to you? How have you responded?

DAY 107: ANOINTED WITH THE OIL OF JOY

TODAY'S READING: PSALM 45:1–9

KEY VERSE: PSALM 45:7

You love righteousness and hate wickedness; therefore God, your God, has set you above your companions by anointing you with the oil of joy.

REFLECTION

The introductory words of Psalm 45 describe it as a wedding song, but this psalm is not merely depicting the wedding of a commoner. This is the wedding of a king. Wait, no, this is not just any king, this is *the* King of Kings and Lord of Lords (see Revelation 17:14). There is none like him in heaven or on earth.

The New Testament writer of the book of Hebrews quotes directly from this psalm: "But about the Son he says, 'Your throne, O God, will last for ever and ever; a scepter of justice will be the scepter of your kingdom. You have loved righteousness and hated wickedness; therefore God, your God, has set you above your companions by anointing you with the oil of joy'" (Hebrews 1:8–9).

Of course, Jesus is the Son the writer of Hebrews is referring to. The throne of Christ "will last for ever and ever"—his kingdom reign will never end. How did Jesus come to occupy this exalted position? Though conceived by the Holy Spirit, he was nevertheless fully human. He was subject to the same frailties and temptations that we face.

This psalm tells us Jesus was elevated to the highest throne because he "loved righteousness and hated wickedness"

(v. 7). Can the same be said about you and me? Do we love righteousness? Do we hate what is evil? The same oil of joy is available to those who follow in the footsteps of our Lord.

RESPONSE

Lord God, help me to love what you love and hate what you hate. Anoint me with your joy as I seek to follow you in every aspect of my life. I pray in the name of Jesus. Amen.

YOUR TURN

What do you love? What do you hate? Do some of these things need to change?

DAY 108: THE GALLANT LOVER

TODAY'S READING: PSALM 45:10–17

KEY VERSE: PSALM 45:11

Let the king be enthralled by your beauty; honor him, for he is your lord.

REFLECTION

If we interpret Psalm 45 as a messianic psalm, as most Bible scholars do, then it logically follows that Jesus is the royal bridegroom and the church is his chosen bride. For reasons we cannot fathom, the King has fallen in love with us. Now this would make sense if we possessed some godly characteristic or showed some inclination to holiness. But the Scripture declares that "while we were still sinners, Christ died for us" (Romans 5:8).

I am reminded of some romance novel, where the gallant lover takes off his coat and lays it in the mud so that his lady love can step across a puddle without soiling her shoes. Jesus is that gallant lover, except he did more than lay down his coat. He lay down his life that we might cross from death to life. Now that's true romance! Jesus has romanced us into his kingdom, and I for one, am forever grateful.

Listen to the psalmist's advice, "Listen, daughter, and pay careful attention: Forget your people and your father's house. Let the king be enthralled by your beauty; honor him, for he is your lord" (Psalm 45:10–11).

If you have bowed your knees at the foot of the cross, he is your Lord. Be beautiful for him, for you are his betrothed. The apostle Paul reminds us of this truth with these words of admonition: "I am jealous for you with a godly jealousy. I promised you to one husband, to Christ, so that I might present you as a pure virgin to him" (2 Corinthians 11:2).

Having been redeemed by Christ, it's now time to make yourself presentable before him, the eternal lover of your soul. Beauty of character is what he appreciates most in his bride.

RESPONSE

Lord God, I want to be beautiful for Jesus. I make it my aim to please you today in all I say, think, and do. I am forever grateful for your love. Amen.

YOUR TURN

In what ways can you make yourself beautiful for the King? What character qualities do you think our Savior would appreciate most?

DAY 109: OUR REFUGE AND STRENGTH

TODAY'S READING: PSALM 46:1–7

KEY VERSE: PSALM 46:1

God is our refuge and strength, an ever-present help in trouble.

REFLECTION

Why are you confident? Confidence is a key ingredient in the life of any child of God. If we lack confidence, we lack faith. In fact, the word confidence is rooted in faith. *Confidence* is derived from the Latin word *fide,* which means faith. It is etymologically linked to words like fidelity and fiduciary—words that stand for trust and true faithfulness. But the faithfulness, fidelity, and confidence we have as a child of God comes as a result of a relationship.

If we have no relationship with someone, how can we trust them? How can we have confidence in them or their actions if we don't know them?

Here in Psalm 46, the psalmist expresses his complete confidence in God. He expresses that confidence despite the evidence around him. Hear his confident assertion: "God is our refuge and strength, an ever-present help in trouble. Therefore we will not fear, though the earth give way and the mountains fall into the heart of the sea, though its waters roar and foam and the mountains quake with their surging" (vv. 1–3).

There is nothing quite as unnerving as an earthquake. I know this from personal experience. When the solid ground beneath one's feet suddenly gives way and rolls and buckles, nerves begin to snap. But the psalmist remains confident because he knows the One who is in control—the One who remains unmoved and unshakable. In times of trouble, we can turn to God.

However, we should not turn to God simply as a last resort. He is the God who is with us always. Our confidence grows as we live with him day by day, in good times and bad. Our confidence grows as we experience him as our rock of refuge and our shelter in the storm. Then we can say, "The LORD Almighty is with us; the God of Jacob is our fortress" (v. 7).

RESPONSE

Lord God, I put my trust in you. In times of trouble you have been my help and my strength. I turn to you in confidence because you are with me. You are my Savior and my God. Amen.

YOUR TURN

Has your confidence been shaken recently? Where have you turned for help?

DAY 110: LEARNING TO BE STILL

TODAY'S READING: PSALM 46:8–11

KEY VERSE: PSALM 46:10

He says, "Be still, and know that I am God; I will
be exalted among the nations, I will be exalted
in the earth."

REFLECTION

As I sit to write this it's Holy Week—a week of
contemplation leading to Good Friday—leading to our
Savior's death on the cross. The opening line of this reading
from Psalm 46 grabs me: "Come and see what the LORD has
done" (v. 8a).

Yes. "Come and see what the LORD has done!" Come
and see what has happened to God's Son. Come and see
"the desolations he has brought on the earth" (v. 8b), the
desolations he has brought on the dust-formed bundle of
flesh that at birth was laid in a manger. Now he is laid on a
cross. He is not wrapped in swaddling clothes. He is stripped
naked, arms pried wide open, and nailed to a cross.

Come and see what has happened to him. This is the
Lord's doing. This is the Father's will. This is the Son's
willing obedience. Now hear the Spirit's beckoning call,
"Come and see what the LORD has done!"

This is what love looks like—not our love for God, but
God's love for man. Love looks like Jesus on the cross. Love
looks like a bloody sacrifice, engineered by God, inflicted

on God, God come-in-the-flesh. Love looks painful—painful because it gives to the last drop. It calls us near to the last breath. "Come and see what the LORD has done!"

And when you come, be still. "He says, 'Be still, and know that I am God'" (v. 10).

Eve reached for the forbidden fruit. Adam rushed after her. Yet this is not the time to rush by. Rushing has brought us this mess—this messed up world, this mess on the cross. Self-centered rushing hurtles us into sin with no thought for tomorrow—no thought for the man on a cross. Instead today, "Be still, and know that I am God; I will be exalted among the nations, I will be exalted in the earth" (v. 10).

Be still. Be still before the cross. He is God. The man on the cross is God. Love has a price, always has a price. It's written in blood—the Savior's blood.

RESPONSE

Lord God, alter me at the foot of the cross. I need you to change my heart, my life, my attitude. Help me be still before you as I contemplate your love—love that I don't deserve, that I have not earned. But Jesus, you offered yourself freely. Thank you. Amen.

YOUR TURN

Has your life been altered by the cross? How has a journey to the cross changed how you live your daily life?

DAY 111: RESURRECTION VICTORY!

TODAY'S READING: PSALM 47

KEY VERSE: PSALM 47:5

God has ascended amid shouts of joy, the LORD amid the sounding of trumpets.

REFLECTION

I appreciate God's timing—it brings a smile to my face. Yesterday's psalm reading seemed particularly appropriate as we reflected on the events of Good Friday. Today's psalm reading is fitting as we rejoice in the triumph of the resurrection. I can't help but think of the risen Christ as I read these words, "God has ascended amid shouts of joy, the LORD amid the sounding of trumpets" (v. 5).

Psalm 47 calls forth a spontaneous joy. It is a song of celebration to the Lord for the victories of the Lord. He has conquered! What has he conquered? The Lord has conquered the nations. "Sing praises to God, sing praises; sing praises to our King, sing praises. For God is the King of all the earth; sing to him a psalm of praise. God reigns over the nations; God is seated on his holy throne" (vv. 6–8).

In its original context, Psalm 47 celebrated the victory of Israel over the surrounding nations. But that is a feeble victory compared to Christ the King's triumph over death, hell, and the power of the grave. Hallelujah! The King is alive. He arose from the dead. The power of sin and Satan are defeated, and because he lives and reigns, we, too, will live and reign with him through eternity. "For if, while we were God's enemies, we were reconciled to him through the death of his Son, how much more, having been reconciled, shall we be saved through his life!" (Romans 5:10).

In the resurrection of Jesus, we have the ultimate cause for celebration. "Shout to God with cries of joy!" (Psalm 47:1).

RESPONSE

Lord God, I thank you for the victory of Jesus! He is my forerunner. I will live and reign through him. Amen.

YOUR TURN

The resurrection means the dead in Christ will be raised. Who will you want to greet first?

DAY 112: THE CITY OF GOD

TODAY'S READING: PSALM 48:1–8

KEY VERSE: PSALM 48:1

Great is the LORD, and most worthy of praise, in the city of our God, his holy mountain.

REFLECTION

I grew up on a farm in wide-open, rural Saskatchewan, Canada. It was a cross-country mile to the nearest neighbor, but if you stood at the right spot in our farmyard, you could see our neighbor's house. I loved growing up on the farm, and I still love visiting. Who wouldn't? I was living in God's country surrounded by the wild beauty of nature in all its varied, changing forms.

But I have spent the last forty years living in the city. Actually, I've lived in three rather large cities with populations of more than a million. Is the God of the open country the God of the city too? The psalmist seemed to think so. He begins Psalm 48 with this declaration, "Great is the LORD, and most worthy of praise, in the city of our God, his holy mountain."

Of course, the sons of Korah were referring to biblical Jerusalem, more specifically Mount Zion, the fortified citadel within the walls of ancient Israel's capital. God was within her. During the reign of David, the Ark of the Covenant—the seat of the Lord's rule—was housed in the sacred tabernacle on Mount Zion. This was where God dwelt.

Where does God dwell today? As partakers of the new covenant, we are the temples of God through the blood of Christ. The apostle Paul asks, "Don't you know that you yourselves are God's temple and that God's Spirit dwells in your midst?" (1 Corinthians 3:16). God dwells in the city too—your city. Whether it's Ottawa, Albuquerque, New York, or Tokyo, God is within her because his redeemed people live there.

RESPONSE

Lord, I thank you because your Spirit lives within us! Help me to let my light shine in my city. Amen.

YOUR TURN

How would you characterize your city? How is God revealing his presence there?

DAY 113: MY CITYSCAPE

TODAY'S READING: PSALM 48:9–14

KEY VERSES: PSALM 48:12–13

Walk about Zion, go around her, count her towers, consider well her ramparts, view her citadels, that you may tell of them to the next generation.

REFLECTION

Have you watched a television newscast recently? Invariably, at some point during that telecast, you will see a cityscape—a grand view of the city skyline in all its glory. Experts being interviewed almost always appear against the backdrop of a large photo of their city. Routinely, sports telecasts feature brief live shots of the arena and the host city's downtown.

Why do broadcasters go to the trouble of filming these cityscapes and providing these skyline backdrops? A good part of the answer is identification. We identify a city by its skyline and by its landmark buildings and towers. Washington, DC, is intimately linked to pictures of the Capitol and the White House, Paris with the Eiffel Tower, and Toronto with the CN Tower. When the twin towers of the World Trade Center were destroyed, New York mourned not only the loss of lives, but also the loss of the twin icons of its identity.

Psalm 48 is the Bible's version of a cityscape telecast. Read the psalmist's call, "Walk about Zion, go around her, count her towers, consider well her ramparts, view her citadels that you may tell of them to the next generation" (vv. 12–13).

What is the psalmist asking us to do? He is asking us to identify with the city of God. What makes Zion unique in the earth is the presence of God within her. The psalmist clearly states, "God is in her citadels" (v. 3). Is God's Spirit within you? Does the Lord reign in your heart and mind? Is he the master of your affections? Have you had landmark experiences with God that changed the course of your life? Have you climbed towers of prayer? Have you stood guard on the ramparts of your mind? Then, with conviction, you can say with the psalmist, "For this God is our God forever and ever; he will be our guide even to the end" (v. 14).

RESPONSE

Lord God, reign in me. Establish your capital in my heart. Govern my ways, now and forevermore. I commit my thoughts and intellect to your service. Stir my heart and my affections. Amen.

YOUR TURN

Has Jesus come to rule your heart? Is the Lord enthroned there? What steps can you take to firmly establish the Lord as the ruler of your mind?

DAY 114: THE PSALMIST GETS IT WRONG!

TODAY'S READING: PSALM 49:1–12

KEY VERSE: PSALM 49:7

No one can redeem the life of another or give to God a ransom for them.

REFLECTION

This opening portion of Psalm 49 reminds me of that old maxim: There are only two certainties in this life—death and taxes. The same fate awaits us all. No one is spared. The Grim Reaper cuts down all without exception. The psalmist asserts the obvious: "For all can see that the wise die, that the foolish and the senseless also perish, leaving their wealth to others" (v. 10).

However, the psalmist is not entirely correct. He makes a sweeping statement that fails to account for a most unusual exception. The psalmist states, "No one can redeem the life of another or give to God a ransom for them—the ransom for a life is costly, no payment is ever enough—so that they should live on forever and not see decay" (vv. 7–9).

Jesus Christ is that unusual exception. He proves the psalmist wrong. Jesus paid my ransom. He redeemed my life. He went to the cross on my behalf and there he poured out his life blood, so accepting that sacrifice, I might live forever. Then, to prove Jesus's sacrifice was accepted, God the Father raised Jesus from the dead. Death no longer has dominion over him. Better still, those who put their trust in

Jesus Christ will be raised to life on the last day. Praise be to God, who breaks the bonds of death.

RESPONSE

Lord, I thank you for the victory of Jesus! By faith, I will live and reign through him. Lord Jesus, you are my redeemer. I rejoice in your great love. Eternity is mine. I am forever grateful. Amen.

YOUR TURN

Jesus faced death and overcame. How can you be an overcomer too, through him?

DAY 115: TWO FATES—ONE CHOICE

TODAY'S READING: PSALM 49:13–20

KEY VERSE: PSALM 49:15

But God will redeem me from the realm of the dead; he will surely take me to himself.

REFLECTION

Throughout Psalm 49, the psalmist is establishing a contrast between those who trust in themselves and the wealth they have accumulated, and those who put their trust in God. Death is the fate of all—rich and poor, wise and foolish. The grave spares no one.

"This is the fate of those who trust in themselves, and of their followers, who approve their sayings. They are like sheep and are destined to die; death will be their shepherd (but the upright will prevail over them in the morning)" (vv. 13–14).

I find great hope between the parentheses in the passage above. "But the upright will prevail over them in the morning." A new day is coming—a day of resurrection—a day where justice will prevail at last. We can rest in hope that wrongs will be righted, truth will triumph over lies, and joy will snuff out sorrow. Yes, a new morning will dawn. A Redeemer is coming. Along with suffering Job, believers can say, "I know that my redeemer lives, and that in the end he will stand on the earth. And after my skin has been destroyed, yet in my flesh I will see God" (Job 19:25–26).

The psalmist boldly declares where he has placed his faith. "But God will redeem me from the realm of the dead; he will surely take me to himself" (Psalm 49:15).

Have you placed your faith, your trust, in Jesus, the Redeemer, who purchased your redemption with his shed blood? Death is a certainty, but so is redemption for those who put their trust in the One who died and rose again.

RESPONSE

Lord God, I thank you that Jesus, my Redeemer, lives! I put my trust in you, now and for eternity. I rest in the hope that a new day will dawn when the dead in Christ will rise. Amen.

YOUR TURN

Is your heart ready for that glorious day? Have you bowed before your Redeemer? How will you respond to him when he takes you home to glory?

DAY 116: THE GREAT SUMMONING!

TODAY'S READING: PSALM 50:1–6

KEY VERSE: PSALM 50:1

The Mighty One, God, the LORD, speaks and summons the earth from the rising of the sun to where it sets.

REFLECTION

Psalm 50 begins by reminding us that Judgment Day is coming. A great summoning will take place. We will all gather before the throne of God. Rich and poor, the powerful and the weak, the living and the dead—all will gather before the Lord. None will be excused. "The Mighty One, God, the LORD, speaks and summons the earth from the rising of the sun to where it sets."

On the day before his crucifixion, Jesus elaborated at some length on this great summoning. For some, this day will be a day of joy and gladness. For others, it will be a day of dread and sorrow. "When the Son of Man comes in his glory, and all the angels with him, he will sit on his glorious throne. All the nations will be gathered before him, and he will separate the people one from another as a shepherd separates the sheep from the goats. He will put the sheep on his right and the goats on his left" (Matthew 25:31–33).

What kind of day will it be for you?

Judgment Day will certainly be a day of justice. Since the fall of man, the world has cried out for justice. All too often in this world—in this life—there is no such thing. The innocent suffer while the perpetrators get off free. They gloat in their pride while swaddled in luxury. On that great day—that Judgment Day—the tables will be turned. The great Judge of all the earth will see to that. And so he should.

In his account of Judgment Day, Jesus decides if we will enter into bliss or torment based on how we treat others. He states, "The King will reply, 'Truly I tell you, whatever you did for one of the least of these brothers and sisters of mine, you did for me'" (Matthew 25:40).

RESPONSE

Lord God, help me to live my life in joyous preparation for that great summoning when wrong will be made right. Help me to be merciful so I will receive your mercy through Jesus. Amen.

YOUR TURN

How can we prepare our hearts and live our lives aright in the knowledge that Judgment Day is coming?

DAY 117: THE SACRIFICE OF THANKSGIVING

TODAY'S READING: PSALM 50:7–15

KEY VERSES: PSALM 50:14–15

"Sacrifice thank offerings to God, fulfill your vows to the Most High, and call on me in the day of trouble; I will deliver you, and you will honor me."

REFLECTION

What is humanity's greatest sin? Is it murder? Hatred? Racism? The desecration of the planet? All of these are serious problems—serious sins. But what is the *greatest* sin?

Psalm 50 begins with a great summoning of all nations. The Lord is about to enter into judgment. But what charge does he bring against his people? He does not accuse them of heinous crimes, or the desecration of his temple. "I bring no charges against you concerning your sacrifices or concerning your burnt offerings, which are ever before me" (v. 8).

Instead, God calls for thank offerings. The Lord wants his people to have thankful hearts. "Sacrifice thank offerings to God, fulfill your vows to the Most High" (v. 14). There is something rather anticlimactic about this call for thanksgiving. My initial reaction was one of surprise. I thought we had a serious problem here. Why summon the nations to a great gathering unless there is coming a declaration of some significance? Surely a lack of thanksgiving is an offense of no great significance. Or is it? Apparently, in God's view it is of great importance.

In his epistle to the Romans, Paul attributes a lack of thankfulness to the blinding power and deception of sin. "For since the creation of the world God's invisible qualities—his eternal power and divine nature—have been clearly seen, being understood from what has been made, so that people are without excuse. For although they knew God, they neither glorified him as God nor gave thanks to him, but their thinking became futile and their foolish hearts were darkened" (Romans 1:20–21).

Because of its long-term consequences, a failure to offer thanks may be the gravest sin of all.

RESPONSE

Lord God, I owe my life to you. I have so much to be thankful for. Every day is a gift. Amen.

YOUR TURN

What are you most thankful for? Why do you think ingratitude has such dire consequences?

DAY 118: FORGETTING GOD

TODAY'S READING: PSALM 50:16–23

KEY VERSE: PSALM 50:23

Those who sacrifice thank offerings honor me,
and to the blameless I will show my salvation.

REFLECTION

I tend to be forgetful. As I leave the house, it is not uncommon for me to forget some rather important items such as my wallet or my mobile phone. On our recent trip to Japan, my wife would often help me run through a checklist of essential items as we set out on an excursion. Wallet, rail pass, mobile phone, and passport—all were needed. I dared not forget any of these.

But there is something more important than all of these "essentials." In his conclusion to Psalm 50, the psalmist Asaph reminds us not to forget God. How often have you set out on your day only to realize you forgot God at home? Maybe he's still at church.

Forgetting God is no small matter. Here is the Lord's response to those who forget him: "Consider this, you who forget God, or I will tear you to pieces, with no one to rescue you: Those who sacrifice thank offerings honor me, and to the blameless I will show my salvation" (vv. 22–23).

We all want to see the salvation of God, but it starts with not forgetting him. When we do, we run the risk of becoming objects of his wrath. The wrath of God is not a popular topic these days, but a lack of popularity does not negate its reality. When we choose to ignore God, there are unpleasant consequences. This applies personally and nationally. When we turn our back on the author of our salvation, terrible things happen. When we embrace him with thanksgiving, joy will be our portion.

RESPONSE

Lord God, let me never forget your great love for me. I want to take you with me today and every day. I am thankful for the promise of your presence. Amen.

YOUR TURN

Do you sometimes forget God as you begin your day? Have you had God with you lately? Have you forgotten him completely as you went about your business?

DAY 119: THE REPENTANT HEART

TODAY'S READING: PSALM 51:1–9

KEY VERSE: PSALM 51:4

Against you, you only, have I sinned and done what is evil in your sight; so you are right in your verdict and justified when you judge.

REFLECTION

Psalm 51 is the great repentance psalm. Nothing matches the deep contrition expressed here by David. There can be little doubt David was truly remorseful for what he had done. He says it with words, but according to the Scriptures, his actions after also revealed a repentant heart. There is no blame shifting here—David takes full responsibility for his actions. Hear his humble plea, "For I know my transgressions and my sin is always before me. Against you, you only, have I sinned and done what is evil in your sight; so you are right in your verdict and justified when you judge" (vv. 3–4).

When Saul and Jonathan were slain in battle by the Philistines, David composed this lament. "Your glory, O Israel, lies slain upon your high places! How the mighty have fallen!" (2 Samuel 1:19 NRSV). David might well have sung this lament for himself. Here he was, the vaunted King of Israel, the Lord's anointed, and he had a fellow soldier murdered to cover up the adulterous affair he was having with this loyal soldier's wife. This was the conduct of David—the man of God! Yes. "How the mighty have fallen!"

The amazing part of this story is not David's sin or the depths of his depravity. The amazing part is that he repented—earnestly repented. In our day, leader after leader has been caught red-handed in unscrupulous practices, but they seldom repent. Do they come clean and change their ways? Not likely. Most often they continue in denial. Those with absolute power continue to govern ruthlessly. Nathan, the prophet, was fortunate that King David paid heed to the voice of God speaking through a human vessel. Rather than hide his sin and silence the prophet, David was quick to humble himself and repent.

RESPONSE

Lord God, I want to be like David—quick to acknowledge my sin and repent. Grant me a soft heart—a sensitive heart—a repentant heart in the name of Jesus. Amen.

YOUR TURN

How do you respond when confronted with your sin? How can we maintain a repentant heart before God? What hinders repentance?

DAY 120: A CLEAN HEART

TODAY'S READING: PSALM 51:10–19

KEY VERSE: PSALM 51:10

Create in me a pure heart, O God, and renew a steadfast spirit within me.

REFLECTION

I just had my morning shower. Nothing special about that—daily showers are the social norm. However, they haven't always been the norm. Step back a century and a *weekly* bath was the norm. Step back a thousand years and a bath was an *annual* event. With this lack of personal hygiene, is it any wonder that epidemics ran rampant through the medieval population, and diseases like smallpox and the bubonic plague killed millions in Europe?

As a society, we have embraced the concept and practice of personal hygiene. But what about spiritual hygiene? Have we embraced that as well? I fear the opposite is true. Are we routinely plunging into the deep end of a cesspool of sin? Do we mistakenly believe there are no consequences? A filthy spirit can be as deadly as bubonic plague. A host of mental, emotional, and social problems are a direct result of poor spiritual hygiene. Cleanse your heart and mind and you will walk in spiritual health.

From his own cesspool of sin, David cried out, "Create in me a pure heart, O God, and renew a steadfast spirit within me. Do not cast me from your presence or take your Holy Spirit from me. Restore to me the joy of your salvation and grant me a willing spirit, to sustain me" (vv. 10–12).

I don't know about you, but I need to bathe daily in Christ's love and forgiveness. He cleans me up.

RESPONSE

Lord God, thank you for the forgiveness you purchased for me through the shed blood of Jesus, your Son. I acknowledge my need for your cleansing power. Amen.

YOUR TURN

How is your spiritual hygiene today? How do you keep your spirit clean?

ABOUT THE AUTHOR

David Kitz is a Bible dramatist, an award-winning author, and a conference speaker. For thirty years, he has served as an ordained minister with the Foursquare Gospel Church of Canada.

David has a Master's degree in Biblical Studies in addition to Bachelor's degrees in both Arts and Education. His love for drama and storytelling is evident to all who have seen his Bible-based performances. For several years now, he has toured across Canada and the United States with a variety of one man plays for both children and adults. Though born and raised in Saskatchewan, David now lives in Ottawa, Canada, with his wife, Karen. They have two adult sons, Timothy and Joshua.

He can be contacted directly at david@davidkitz.ca

ENDNOTES:

1 Park, Alice, "Take That! Athletes' Victory Stances Are All About Dominance, Not Pride," Time, January 10, 2014, http://time.com/464/take-that-athletes-victory-stances-are-all-about-dominance-not-pride.

2 Hayford, Jack W., ed., Spirit Filled Life Bible: A Personal Study Bible Unveiling All God's Fullness in All God's Word (New King James Version), Nashville, TN: Thomas Nelson Inc., 1991, 768.

3 Hanover College, "Lord Acton (John Emerich Edward Dalberg) Letter to Archbishop Mandell Creighton," accessed July 1, 2020, https://history.hanover.edu/courses/excerpts/165acton.html.

4 Gladwell, Malcolm, David and Goliath, France: Little, Brown and Company, 2013.

5 MacMillan, Margaret, The War That Ended Peace, The Road to 1914, New York: Random House, 2013.

6 Ortberg, John, Know Doubt: The Importance of Embracing Uncertainty in Your Faith, Nashville, TN: Zondervan, 2008, 87.

Manufactured by Amazon.ca
Bolton, ON